HISTORY FOR
WITH LEARNING
DIFFICULTIES

M. D. Wilson, MA, MEd

Deputy Head
Carr Hill High School, Kirkham

HODDER AND STOUGHTON
LONDON SYDNEY AUCKLAND TORONTO

British Library Cataloguing in Publication Data

Wilson, M. D.
  History for pupils with learning difficulties.
  1. History——Study and teaching (Secondary)
  ——Great Britain   2. Slow learning children——
  Great Britain
  I. Title
  371.92′64   D16.4.G7

ISBN 0 340 35949 8

First published 1985

Typeset by Macmillan India Ltd., Bangalore.
Printed by Page Bros. (Norwich) Ltd.
for Hodder and Stoughton Educational, a division of Hodder and Stoughton Ltd,
Mill Road, Dunton Green, Sevenoaks, Kent

Contents

Introduction and Acknowledgements

The origins of this study are to be found in research conducted at the University of Exeter in 1979 to 1980. It was a time when the education of pupils with learning difficulties was becoming an issue of major concern and interest in specific subject areas. Rapid developments have certainly taken place over the past five years.

It is the aim of this book to piece together various strands of educational research, the ideas and recommendations of practising teachers, and discussion on new classroom materials and approaches to teaching. It is not intended to be an overly prescriptive teachers' guide or manual. The purpose is rather to provide a comprehensive discussion, with a view to stimulating further refinement and innovation, both in schools and institutes of higher education, particularly those with an interest in teacher training. The fundamental importance of school-based innovation and evaluation is stressed throughout. Although the book deals specifically with the teaching of history to children with learning difficulties, it should be of interest to all teachers of history. It should also be of value to those teachers who have a particular interest in, or responsibility for, special educational needs in the comprehensive school.

In preparing the groundwork for my research, I gratefully acknowledge the help received from staff of the University of Exeter Faculty of Education. My thanks are due to Dr Jon Nichol (Lecturer in Education) for encouragement and advice throughout; to Dr Kay Woods (formerly Research Assistant) for advice and the loan of some valuable material; to Colin McCall, HMI (formerly Lecturer in Education) for drawing my attention to a number of valuable references and generously lending me a typescript article prior to publication; to Dr Peter Gurney (Lecturer in Education) who kindly commented on my questionnaires and saved me from several errors of design and to Dr M. B. Booth (University of Cambridge Department of Education) for his illuminating comments and constructive criticism of the typescript. Of course, the responsibility for any remaining faults must be mine.

I should also like to thank several people who gave me expert advice on computer-assisted learning, namely Frances Blow, Trinity and All Saints' College, Leeds; M. Barton of the Microelectronics Education Development Unit, Lincolnshire; and Dr Jon Nichol, University of Exeter.

Finally, I should like to express my deep gratitude to all the head teachers, teaching staff and pupils of the schools in my various surveys. Without their kind co-operation in completing the questionnaires, discussing their syllabuses and allowing my access to highly confidential files, this study would not have been possible. A special thank-you is also due to my colleague, Margaret Fenton, of the Humanities Department, Carr Hill High School, for permission to reproduce the European Studies profile in Appendix D.

Michael Wilson, Kirkham

1

The Child with Learning Difficulties

INTRODUCTION

There is evidence to suggest – evidence which will unfold in subsequent chapters – that educational provision for children of low academic attainment, particularly in specialist subject areas, is far from satisfactory. A fundamental problem has been the lack of any agreed definition of the child with special educational needs, because without such a definition there can be no clear strategy of remediation. It is to this problem that we turn first.

THE PROBLEM OF DEFINITION

Any discussion of pupils with learning difficulties runs into the difficulty of definition and the associated problem of labelling. There has been no shortage of terms to describe such children, but there has been considerable divergence and inconsistency in their usage[1]. Most of the labels have also been criticised for a number of reasons:

1 Epithets such as 'retarded' and 'backward' are hurtful and acquire some form of stigma
2 Labels tend to categorise pupils, with the mistaken inference on the part of teachers that the children form a relatively homogeneous group. Terms such as ESN (educationally sub-normal) and even 'slow learner' suggest some intrinsic deficiency for what could be social or cultural disadvantage. Not all low achievers are slow learners; their disappointing level of attainment may well result from lack of motivation or from prolonged absences from school and serious gaps in knowledge
3 The act of labelling seems inevitably to lead to a self-fulfilling prophecy, whereby children who are clearly marked out as being dull develop a poor self-image and quickly conform to their teachers' limited expectations
4 Such categories provide little assistance in determining the pedagogic needs of children with learning difficulties.

There is something to be said for the view that too much time is spent defining problems rather than presenting solutions. However, a clear conception of the various learning difficulties is a necessary foundation for a carefully structured remedial programme which can help low achievers to cope more effectively with their learning problems.

The Warnock Report (1978) into special education made wide and far-reaching recommendations. The Committee claimed that the 'vast majority' of children requiring special educational provision were to be found in the classrooms of ordinary schools, and that this was where their needs should be met. The Report suggested a three-fold classification according to the degree of learning handicap; that is to say, children whose learning difficulties are:

1 *Mild* – the largest single group of children needing special provision, including most remedial children in ordinary schools
2 *Moderate* – the so-called ESN children, most of whom will be in special schools
3 *Severe* – the mentally handicapped.

The extent of the problem in ordinary schools has been under-estimated. A typical remedial or withdrawal class will accommodate the least able five per cent to ten per cent of the year group, and yet the Warnock Report estimated that up to twenty per cent of children could require special educational provision at some time during their school careers. Put another way, as many as six pupils could require specialist help in an average mixed-ability class of thirty[2]. Furthermore, the proportion of children of below-average academic ability (i.e. those unlikely to achieve any appreciable success in external examinations at sixteen plus) could be as high as forty per cent in some schools. Although the majority of these pupils are unlikely to be regarded as slow learners, they share many of their problems, but to a lesser degree. For example:

1 They may have learning difficulties in such crucial areas as reading and writing, but their problems are rarely considered serious enough to attract specialist attention
2 They are likely to share a sense of scholastic failure, and as a result may be poorly motivated, especially in the more academic subjects
3 They are almost certain to receive a separate curriculum, especially at fourteen plus, when the majority of pupils embark on external examination courses
4 Their teachers are likely to encounter difficulty in sustaining interest and motivation in the more academic subjects. One major reason for this is the paucity of suitable curricular materials that are simple linguistically and conceptually, and yet mature and interesting in content and presentation.

The most suitable definitions are those which are broad and non-categorical. We are then made aware that pupils with special educational needs are far from homogeneous, but encapsulate an almost infinite range of educational problems. Our focus of attention must then be very much on the specific learning difficulties and educational needs of the individual child. Thus, both the Warnock Report and the 1981 Education Act (Special Educational Needs) recommend the use of the term 'children with learning difficulties'[3]. These children may also be regarded as *low achievers*, in the sense that they are unable to cope successfully with work in school which is considered normal for their age group. The term 'low achiever' is purely descriptive (on the evidence of school performance), with no implied aetiology. Consequently, throughout the course of this study, the expressions 'children with learning difficulties' and 'low achievers' will be used interchangeably.

Such blanket definitions obviously subsume a wide range of learning difficulties, which can now be examined in more detail.

LEARNING DIFFICULTIES: AN OVERVIEW

Although low achievers do not constitute a homogeneous group, it is common practice in most comprehensive schools to allocate the least able pupils to a single remedial class. This usually has the great benefit of a more favourable pupil–teacher ratio, but there is a danger that the curriculum offered lacks the necessary diversity to meet adequately individual needs. This is particularly true in the case of lessons taught by subject specialists who lack training and/or experience in remedial education. Brennan argues that schools need to offer three basic types of curriculum if individual needs are to be met more effectively. However, the 'three kinds of education are neither independent nor sequential but interact and create a situation which can be resolved through the provision of balanced, individual curricular programmes.'[4] From the three types of curriculum recommended, it is possible to identify three broad areas of learning difficulty. ˊ

1 SEVERELY LIMITED GENERAL ABILITY

Children in this category display a very low level of achievement in all tested areas, their IQ ratings usually being below 85. In ordinary schools they are likely to be labelled 'remedial' or 'slow learner'; in special schools 'educationally sub-normal'. In the words of Colin McCall: 'Accepting the limitations of standardised tests and remembering the problems of the predictive validity of tests and the disadvantages of too rapidly applying labels, etc – nevertheless it seems fair to comment that such youngsters exist'.[5] Their deficiencies have some degree of permanence, including some or all of the following: a low level of intellectual competence, perceptual immaturity, difficulty with concept formation and sequential thought, difficulty in acquiring new knowledge or skills, a low level of general awareness, and continually shifting interest and attention. The more extreme cases will require placement in a special school, although the Warnock Report has recommended more integration of children with special educational needs into the mainstream of education provided in ordinary schools. In Piagetian terms, the so-called ESN children are likely to function at the level of preoperational or intuitive thought. Although their vocabulary may be substantial, their thinking is not rational, they explain physical phenomena animistically, their judgements are based on personal feelings rather than rules or moral principles, and the cause of events cannot be rationally explained but accounted for intuitively: 'It goes without saying that teachers are severely limited in transmitting concepts to a child at this stage, even in a highly intuitive manner.'[6] History, as the term is generally understood, cannot be taught to these children, although historical materials, such as museum artefacts, lively illustrations and good stories could be useful centres of interest. However, most low achievers are likely to have reached the stage of concrete operational thought, typical of children aged 7–11 years. Their thought patterns have become 'operational' in the sense of 'getting data about the real world into the mind and there transforming them so that they can be organised and used selectively in the solutions of problems.'[7] Such children are capable of rational thought, but only when based on concrete experiences. Of course, this has major implications for the way in which history is taught to low achievers. Pupils of very limited general ability 'appear to require special adaptation of the normal school curriculum from the beginning and all through formal education' – that is, an 'adaptive-developmental' curriculum or programme of long-term support[8].

2 SOCIAL DISADVANTAGE

Difficulties generated by limitations of the environment, including gaps in basic knowledge and experiential deprivation in early childhood, seriously affect normal school progress. Research in the 1960's drew attention to inequalities of educational opportunity caused by differences in social class. Professor Bernstein, for example, argued that the restricted use of language in many homes hampers a child's academic progress, not only through acquaintance with a limited vocabulary, but also through experience of only the simplest language structures[9]. Immigrant children may be similarly disadvantaged by their lack of familiarity with English language and culture. As Professor Bernbaum has shown, such problems are particularly significant to the history teacher, whose subject depends heavily on a good command of language:

> The point of note, of course, is that history, along with other cognitive disciplines, is a verbal expression of a unique way of ordering experience. The subject has its own methods, concepts and criteria for truth. Inevitably, these are represented in an elaborated code involving a great deal of qualification, reservation, modification and subordination. It follows . . . therefore that the meanings to be conveyed by the history teacher or the history book may not readily be comprehended by the pupils, and more particularly, the age of the pupils and the social class of the pupils are likely to be important variables relating to the degree of understanding attained.[10]

But differences in social class fail to explain why the majority of working-class children function normally at school. Serious retardation – where this can be attributed to sociological factors – is perhaps more specifically the result of parental neglect or disregard for education. In extreme cases the children will be deprived, distressed and emotionally disturbed. More generally, they are likely to experience such problems as the absence of intellectually stimulating adults, an inadequate language model at home, frequent absences from school, a restricted and unstimulating neighbourhood, and inappropriate or ineffective teaching in school. Disruptive and disaffected schoolchildren are likely to have serious social problems, but these are not confined to low achievers alone[11]. Consequently, it would be inappropriate to digress into an area of educational research which has become highly specialised in its own right[12]. For the socially disadvantaged pupil, Brennan recommends short-term or medium-term object-ives in a learning situation where they can follow a 'corrective-compensatory' curriculum in small groups – 'corrective' in the sense of eliminating inaccurate or inappropriate learning; 'compensatory' in the sense of establishing knowl-edge to fill the gaps in early learning.

3 SPECIFIC LEARNING DISABILITIES

There are pupils with normal intellectual potential and a history of circum-stances conducive to normal learning who fail to make adequate progress. They may suffer from learning disabilities which appear to originate within the pupils themselves:

> The hypothesis is that the disabilities arise from structural or functional inadequacy or abnormality in the neurological systems which conduct sensory information in the system, or in the recall of information as the basis of learning and behaviour.[13]

Problems frequently encountered by these pupils include general clumsiness, perceptual disorders, poor perceptual-motor links (e.g. hand-eye co-ordination), auditory and visual defects, confused thought processes, and specific problems with language or numbers (e.g. developmental dyslexia and dysphasia). It would be both beyond my competence and the scope of this study to comment at length on these problems of abnormal psychology, especially as there are several excellent introductions to the subject[14]. Brennan recommends a withdrawal or 'remedial' curriculum, by which pupils can spend some time each day at an SLD unit and gain expert help with their specific disabilities from a highly trained specialist. It is suggested that these pupils spend the remainder of their timetable following a normal common curriculum and gaining the appropriate intellectual stimulus from integration with the main school. Close and regular liaison between remedial teachers and subject teachers (who are unlikely to have specialist knowledge of specific learning disabilities) is not only highly desirable, but essential.

We can now examine a number of case studies, which provide a more personal and intimate analysis of learning difficulties and serve to illustrate some of the general statements made about low achievers.

PUPIL CASE STUDIES

The following case studies are taken from a research enquiry conducted in 1980[15]. In compiling these pupil profiles, I am greatly indebted to the staff of the schools for allowing me access to school reports and confidential records, including the reports of educational psychologists. Of course, all the names quoted are pseudonyms in order to conceal the identity of the pupils.

Although learning difficulties may be crudely categorised, it can be seen that the combination of problems facing the individual pupil defy satisfactory classification: many low achievers suffer from a multiplicity of learning handicaps. The case studies also serve to illustrate the considerable challenge facing history teachers in comprehensive schools. All four pupils (adolescent boys aged 13–14) were taught history by subject, not remedial, specialists.

1 JOHN

John has an IQ rating of only 81. In Piagetian terms, his thinking is at the level of concrete operations, and his conceptual development is only rudimentary. His definition of history, expressed in terms of concrete associations, illustrates this well: 'Early wars and James Stuart.' On the basis of a pupil questionnaire (Appendix A), John's attitude to school is more negative than the mean response of his peers, and he claims that school is more boring than it was the previous year 'because we can get work that we do not no about' (*sic*). Although he likes history, saying that 'it is interesting because you can learn about many years ago', he makes a similar plea that he finds the subject difficult. Of particular concern to the school is his lack of progress, not to say deterioration, in reading from the evidence of standardised tests (Reading Age 7.8 years in the first year; Reading Age only 7.0 years in the third). Moreover, John has a tendency to bully, and has recent convictions for petty theft and vandalism. Many of his problems would appear to arise from a disadvantaged home background. He never knew his father, who left his mother and six children shortly before his birth. John was first referred to an educational psychologist when he was eight, suffering from enuresis, when it was concluded that his unhappiness and insecurity were clearly external to the school environment:

> In discussion, he spoke positively about school but complained about sibling relationships at home. He said he liked his little sister but disliked all his brothers. He complained that his brothers bullied him and that his mother often smacked him. According to John his mother is often out when he returns home from school and he climbs in through the window. When he lets his brothers in they bully him and make him cry.

John is both socially disadvantaged and severely limited in terms of general ability. His lack of school progress may also have something to do with working in a mixed-ability class, where he is hopelessly at sea, and where the history staff openly admit to their difficulties in coping adequately with individual needs. John would benefit from more individual tutoring and counselling (perhaps on a withdrawal basis) and allocation to a small special class, where he could follow an 'adaptive-developmental' curriculum. His limitations are such that he only narrowly missed placement in a special school.

2 TREVOR

When Trevor left primary school in 1977 his form teacher's report was promising: 'Concentrating harder and making a real effort to improve. Reading and English are rather weak, but a pleasant boy of average ability who is progressing well.' However, his most recent report proliferates with adverse comments, emphasising his negative attitude, not his lack of ability or potential. The report of the history teacher epitomises what has become a tragic case of under-achievement:

> I am sure that if Trevor made a real effort and applied himself, he would not even be in this teaching group. Frequent absences, rather slapdash work and late handing in of work have combined to lower his standard. Some measure of his ability is perhaps gained from his excellent exam result. Nevertheless, I cannot recommend that he take history next year.

In many ways Trevor may be regarded as a low achiever, but not as a slow learner. However, it is not unusual to find children like him in bottom bands or even remedial groups. What has gone wrong in Trevor's case? An estranged father and a mother clearly at the end of her tether appear to account for his basic insecurity, lack of self-discipline and poor school attendance. A recent letter from the mother to the headmaster provides insight into the nature of the boy's underlying anxieties:

> I apologise for Trevor absent from school over the week. If I explain the situation I'm sure you'll understand. A tug of love situation has developed over his younger brother. The child father has more or less grab him from me. The resort of this has been many visit social worker, solicitors ect. This has all be very upsetting to myself and the other children. Trevor being the eldster feels the responsability of helping me and worry's greatly over are unhappiness. (*sic*)

Domestic troubles have eclipsed school from Trevor's list of priorities. With no prospect of taking external examination courses, Trevor's self-esteem and alienation from school may get worse. Although Trevor has had a history of learning difficulties with reading and English, his main problems are clearly social. Recommendations at this stage are far easier than solutions, because Trevor may have already fallen by the wayside. However, the following suggestions could prove beneficial:

(a) close liaison between school, home and the support agencies, perhaps co-ordinated by the pastoral team;
(b) the provision of a crash course on a 'corrective-compensatory' basis, to put right any deficiencies in reading and English, or gaps in knowledge caused by prolonged absences;
(c) the offer of fourth/fifth year courses commensurate with the boy's ability and potential, subject to reasonable effort and satisfactory behaviour.

3 ALEC

Alec is a pleasant, sociable boy with a favourable attitude to school. He likes his teachers and regards most of his subjects as both interesting and important. Alec's most obvious disability, from the evidence of the data, is his very low non-verbal IQ of 58, a consequence of hydrocephalus which resulted in brain cell loss and damage. Alec attends a children's hospital once a week for therapy, but no specific treatment is available for his condition, other than a close one-to-one relationship. Alec's attendance at a comprehensive school complies with his own wishes, the wishes of his parents and the approval of the educational psychologist, who concluded that he would derive benefit from an ordinary classroom situation because of his adequate attainment in reading and conceptual understanding. Alec's low level of non-verbal functioning is evident from the difficulties he encounters with visual perception, eye-hand co-ordination, left – right sequencing and tasks such as fastening buttons and ties – 'difficulties likely to be pervasive in all school work.' Unfortunately, he faced serious problems in settling down in a large comprehensive school:

> Alec suffers taunts and teasing from peers because of clumsiness and his tendency to become lost. His difficulties have been discussed with his class group in the hope that understanding and tolerance will be shown

Alec's problems are a clear example of children with specific learning disabilities. If the recommendations of the Warnock Committee are fully implemented, then we can expect comprehensive schools to be accommodating for more children like Alec. Learning props used by Alec's remedial teacher include mnemonics and the partial coverage of pages to aid visual perception in reading. As aids to developing basic skills, these techniques should also be utilised by Alec's subject teachers. Nowhere is the need for liaison between the remedial and subject departments more apparent.

4 CRAIG

Craig is polite and good-humoured and has a favourable attitude to school. He has a good average verbal IQ, but his visual-motor skills vary considerably. He has problems in writing and sequencing at speed, and has a Reading Age of only 9.0 years. Craig's thinking, movements and verbal responses are literally slow, and he has 'an ingrained avoidance of difficult situations.' Craig's parents (both teachers) are extremely concerned about his lack of progress, and requested the boy's transfer to his present school, which offers boarding facilities. Once Craig was transferred, his former headmaster sent a report to his new school, outlining Craig's difficulties:

> So far as work is concerned, Craig needed almost total adult supervision before he would put pen to paper or even participate in what was going on in the classroom. Left to himself he would be very passive and apparently totally absorbed in his own uncommunicative thoughts . . . .It would seem that Craig's behaviour was very similar in his previous school and his parents feel that perhaps their own

expectations of Craig had been too great at the time. When speaking to a psychiatrist, they said he had 'worn the skin off his lips with anxiety'.

Craig's difficulties are very complex. His poor visual–motor skills suggest specific learning difficulties, which may account for his slowness and lack of progress in reading, but there is much in the headmaster's report to suggest a significant degree of maladjustment. High parental expectations, combined with a growing sense of personal failure, are perhaps largely to blame for deep-rooted psychlogical difficulties, evident in social withdrawal and a reluctance to tackle problems. The dread of making mistakes could be perhaps mollified by allowing Craig time to jot down his ideas in 'rough' and by teachers reducing their emphasis on formal assessment – at least until Craig has had time to build his confidence. Techniques of behaviour modification, designed to improve confidence through encouragement and reward, may also point towards a solution; but therapy of this kind is long-term and highly specialised. At his new school, Craig appears to be settling down as a boarder (away from the pressures of his home environment) and is spending a further twelve months in the third year to ease academic pressures and to allow him time to catch up with his school work.

INTELLIGENCE AND HISTORICAL THINKING

Intelligence has long been regarded as an issue of relevance to any study of pupils of low academic ability, the popular assumption being that such pupils are considerably limited in intelligence. Early research into backwardness and intelligence was characterised by an emphasis on measurement: a belief that intelligence was a faculty that could be measured both accurately and objectively[16].

There is no doubt that these early psychometric tests have been of some assistance in diagnosing learning disabilities; but attempts to measure intelligence, and particularly the belief in a fixed IQ, have been regarded with increasing scepticism over the years. It is for this reason that the NFER devised a Learning Ability Test (the LAT Project) as an alternative form of diagnostic testing: 'The underlying rationale is based on the notion of learning ability rather than intelligence. Instead of measuring what a child knows or has learnt already, the aim is to assess his capacity to learn, his ability to respond to teaching.'[17] The implied distinction between 'intelligence' and 'learning ability' has far-reaching implications. Statistics are an arguably spurious prognosis of learning potential. They may well be responsible for inaccurately dubbing some socially deprived children, or children of ethnic minority groups, as slow learners. The concept of intelligence must be seen more firmly in the context of developmental psychology, the context of learning and the process of education.

Developmental psychology owes much to the pioneering work of Piaget. Although Piaget's stages of cognitive development have been approximated to chronological ages, they perhaps best equate with what might be loosely termed the 'mental age' of pupils; that is to say, their level of intellectual maturity. Professor E. A. Peel has long shown a research interest in Piaget and the development of pupils' thinking in literary subjects, including history, an area of investigation not covered in Piaget's original experiments. Peel has suggested that in history pupils progress through stages of cognitive development closely parallel to those advocated by Piaget[18]. In a recent lecture, he was also to emphasise how chronological age is only one of a number of variables in determining a child's stage of development; ability and the 'readiness potential' of the individual for mastering the next step were other factors mentioned[19]. In a recent research experiment, 720 children and adolescents aged 9–11 years (ninety students in each age group) were asked nine questions on a text about the destruction of Florentine art treasures by serious floods. In all, there were 810 responses for each age group (9×90) and each of these was classified according to a stage of cognitive development. From the following example, it can be seen that Peel's stages relate closely to those of Piaget:

Question: Are the Italians to blame for the loss of the paintings and art treasures?

Responses: (a) No, because they've got lots of treasures.
(Peel – prelogical; Piaget – intuitive/preoperational.)

(b) I don't think they are. I think it was just the weather, and the rain had come.
(Peel – circumstantial/describer; Piaget – concrete operational.)

(c) Well, not entirely, but they were partly because they could have put them somewhere they weren't da-maged by the floods, but if there was nowhere to put then they were not to blame.
(Peel – imaginative/explanatory; Piaget – formal operational.)

The incidence of imaginative/explanatory judgements is summarised in Table 1.1 according to both age and ability levels. It can be seen that acceleration points to higher levels of thought seem to be at the age 11–12 in the case of pupils of higher ability; 12–13 in the case of less able pupils. But at every age the more able children display a far greater propensity for 'imaginative/expla-natory' thinking[20].

There is one important question not answered in the work of Piaget: to what extent can the conceptual development of children be accelerated through effective teaching? In this respect, the work of Bruner has been particularly influential. First, it is essential for the teacher to ascertain the vital features of

Table 1.1   The Incidence of Imaginative-Explanatory Judgements (Peel, 1980)

AGE	NUMBER OF RESPONSES	
	Lower Ability	Higher Ability
9.0	42	136
10.0	61	137
11.0	135	195
12.0	189	366
13.0	368	472
14.0	396	565
15.0	457	573
16.0	531	620

(When the total number of responses for each age group is $9 \times 90 = 810$.)

his subject – the basic knowledge, skills and concepts that are to be learned by the pupils:

> Good teaching that emphasizes the structure of a subject is probably even more valuable for the less able student than for the gifted one, for it is the former rather than the latter who is most easily thrown off the track by poor teaching.[21]

Secondly, it is essential for the teacher to convey the structure of his/her subject in a form which the pupils can readily understand. All too often, an emphasis on literary skills and abstract thinking can disadvantage the child whose forte, if any, is in 'making' and 'doing'. Low achievers usually encounter most difficulty with abstract thought, reading and writing, but intelligence is arguably both 'concrete' and 'abstract'[22]. Low achievers are not always incapable of understanding complex ideas: rather we must enable them to understand in a different way. John Duncan, in expressing his concern for pupils whose verbal and performance quotients showed a marked discrepancy, emphasised the need for teaching methods that encouraged thinking and problem solving through practical activities[23]. This is consistent with Bruner's 'spiral curriculum', whereby a child encounters the key concepts of a subject discipline in forms of varying difficulty, commencing with the simplest and most concrete represen-tations and progressing to the more complex and comprehensive.

Early attempts to establish any correlation between IQ and aptitude in school subjects failed to yield conclusive results. Schonell, for example, was unable to draw any conclusions except that 'other qualities in addition to general intelligence are required for success in school work.'[24] His correlation coefficient for history was 0.58. More recently, Simon and Ward made an attempt to assess the importance of variables such as IQ and Reading Age in affecting the performance of low achievers on Brown's *History Workshop Unit*. The correlations between the history test scores and IQ, and between the history test scores and Reading Age, were 0.67 and 0.66 respectively[25]. Personality was an important variable, the relatively successful children having a high rating for persistence. However, these findings cannot be accepted without reservation.

Not only is IQ a dubious prognosticator of educational performance, but measurements of IQ and Reading Age tend to indicate very specific aptitudes or learning disorders. Moreover, our understanding of the nature of history and its value in the learning processes of children has become far more sophisticated in recent years. Historical thinking, for example, involves far more than analysis, interpretation and deductive reasoning; it also involves imaginative insight and synthesis, 'and this is an activity which demands open-minded, divergent thinking.'[26] This type of thinking, akin to creativity, finds no place in the Piagetian model[27], which, until very recently, structured most of the research into children's concept formation in history. Creativity and imagination are variables of intellect which have not been satisfactorily correlated with IQ.[28]

In relating these theoretical considerations to the classroom situation, it must be remembered that children with a low IQ rating, or problems with reading and writing, may be gifted in other ways, particularly in practical pursuits, such as painting, modelling, drama, role-play and oral work. Opportunities exist for such creative activities in the study of history; and teachers should guard against underestimating the capabilities of pupils with learning difficulties.

PUPIL ATTITUDES AND MOTIVATION

Pupils' attitudes are important because they provide insights into inter-related issues in educational psychology, including personality, self-esteem, motivation and the optimal conditions of learning. The factors which promote the most favourable attitudes, the greatest motivation and the best learning conditions are vital matters for the school curriculum, particularly in a school that has not recognised the need for a multi-cultural curriculum.

Recent investigations into the attitudes of school children to the study of history are extremely valuable, but they tell us little specifically about the attitudes of low achievers; nor do they say much about how history is rated by children alongside other subjects on the timetable[29]. These issues, which were to direct the course of my own enquiry, are of considerable importance for two reasons: first, low achievers are usually regarded as among the least motivated of pupils, and secondly, a comparison of attitudes to different subjects provides a useful perspective, placing history in the wider context of the whole curriculum.

My own study was based on the attitudes of 150 low achievers in three large comprehensive schools. Schools **A** and **B** are located in an industrial town in Lancashire; School **C** in rural Devon[30]. The pupils selected were from the lowest bands, which corresponded to the least able twenty-five per cent of the ability range in School **A**, and the least able fourteen per cent in School **C**. School **B** was organised on a mixed-ability system, so the low achievers were selected according to the assessments (both formal and informal) of their history teachers; they accounted for the least able twenty per cent of the year group. All the pupils in the survey were in their third year (aged 13–14 between 1979 and 1980), because most younger pupils followed integrated humanities courses with no clear conception of history as a separate discipline, and most older students either no longer continued with history, or did so as an optional subject. The three schools differed both in terms of their organisation of pupils of lower ability and in their approaches to history teaching. It was anticipated

Fig. 1.1 Subject Ratings by 150 Low Achievers 1: Interest Criterion
(Aggregate scores, based on a five-point Likert scale, are in the range 150 × 1 to 150 × 5)

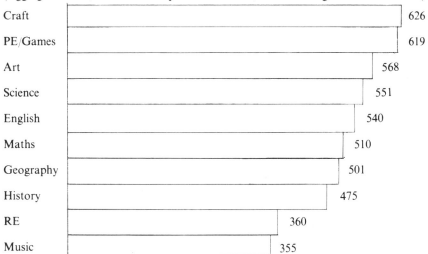

Fig. 1.2 Subject Ratings by 150 Low Achievers 2: Importance Criterion
(Aggregate scores, based on a five-point Likert scale, are in the range 150 × 1 to 150 × 5)

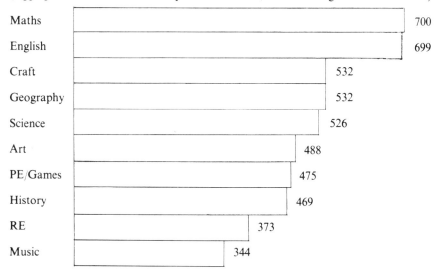

that such differences would help to explain any variations in pupil attitudes between the schools.

Evidence from the three schools indicates that low achievers have a relatively unfavourable attitude to history. Using a five-point Likert scale, pupils were asked to rate each of ten subjects according to how they viewed both their interest and importance. On average, history came eighth – according to both criteria – a calculation based on the aggregate scores for each subject. These are shown diagrammatically in Figures 1.1 and 1.2. The numbers of positive, neutral and negative responses for each school are shown in Tables 1.2 and 1.3. These findings were a close approximation to the earlier survey of the Schools Council in 1968, which concluded that history was second only to religious education in its unpopularity[31]. An unsuitable curriculum is likely to result in

Table 1.2   *Classification of Responses to Subject Ratings 1: According to Interest*

	X	Y	Z		X	Y	Z
ENGLISH				**RE**			
School **A**	49	10	14	School **A**	22	9	42
School **B**	37	6	4	School **B**	8	12	27
School **C**	10	12	8	School **C**	3	8	19
Totals	96	28	26	*Totals*	33	29	88
MATHS				**PE/GAMES**			
School **A**	50	16	7	School **A**	56	11	6
School **B**	24	13	10	School **B**	42	5	0
School **C**	10	8	12	School **C**	20	4	6
Totals	84	37	29	*Totals*	118	20	12
SCIENCE				**ART**			
School **A**	40	19	14	School **A**	53	9	11
School **B**	37	2	8	School **B**	34	6	7
School **C**	19	6	5	School **C**	15	5	10
Totals	96	27	27	*Totals*	102	20	28
HISTORY				**MUSIC**			
School **A**	43	16	14	School **A**	16	10	47
School **B**	11	19	17	School **B**	18	12	17
School **C**	12	10	8	School **C**	4	3	23
Totals	66	45	39	*Totals*	38	25	87
GEOGRAPHY				**CRAFT**			
School **A**	46	15	12	School **A**	55	10	8
School **B**	26	8	13	School **B**	40	5	2
School **C**	12	7	11	School **C**	25	4	1
Totals	84	30	36	*Totals*	120	19	11

Column **X**:   Number of positive responses
Column **Y**:   Number of neutral responses
Column **Z**:   Number of negative responses

Table 1.3 *Classification of Responses to Subject Ratings 2: According to Importance*

	X	Y	Z		X	Y	Z
ENGLISH				**RE**			
School **A**	71	1	1	School **A**	16	17	40
School **B**	46	0	1	School **B**	14	13	20
School **C**	28	2	0	School **C**	12	4	18
Totals	145	3	2	*Totals*	42	34	78
MATHS				**PE/GAMES**			
School **A**	70	3	0	School **A**	37	18	18
School **B**	42	4	1	School **B**	21	15	11
School **C**	27	3	0	School **C**	13	5	12
Totals	139	10	1	*Totals*	71	38	41
SCIENCE				**ART**			
School **A**	40	21	12	School **A**	37	21	15
School **B**	28	14	5	School **B**	32	8	7
School **C**	15	9	6	School **C**	5	12	13
Totals	83	44	23	*Totals*	74	41	35
HISTORY				**MUSIC**			
School **A**	39	23	11	School **A**	11	13	49
School **B**	16	13	18	School **B**	14	16	17
School **C**	9	7	14	School **C**	2	9	19
Totals	64	43	43	*Totals*	27	38	85
GEOGRAPHY				**CRAFT**			
School A	52	10	11	School **A**	38	16	19
School **B**	24	11	12	School **B**	36	6	5
School **C**	16	4	10	School **C**	14	11	5
Totals	92	25	33	*Totals*	88	33	29

Column **X**: Number of positive responses
Column **Y**: Number of neutral responses
Column **Z**: Number of negative responses

boredom rather than enthusiasm, failure rather than success, low self-esteem rather than confidence. An analysis of pupil self-ratings for achievement showed this clearly: forty-five per cent of the low achievers regarded themselves as failures in history, but only twenty-eight per cent believed that they were failing at school in general.

Pupils questioned the relevance of history and claimed that they found the subject too difficult. When asked to suggest improvements to their lessons, the children expressed their dissatisfaction with teaching and learning *methods*. Only in a few cases did the question of subject *content* arise. The most popular request was for more visits, followed by a greater use of audio-visual aids and group discussions (see Table 1.4).

Table 1.4   *Pupil Requests for History Lessons (Based on 150 Low Achievers)*

REQUEST	Col. 1	Col. 2
More visits/fieldwork	84	1
More films	23	2
More drawing activity	17	3
Less writing activity	12	4
More practical work	9	5
Better/more choice of textbooks	8	6=
More work on the history of war	8	6=
More topic/project work	7	8
More work on recent history	6	9
Less teacher talk	5	10=
More work on local history	5	10=

Column 1: Number of times requested
Column 2: Rank order of frequency

Although the overall rating of history by low achievers was low, totals and averages obscure significant differences between the three schools. This is shown in Table 1.5. Clearly the low achievers in School **A** had the most favourable attitude to history. Even the very least able of this group (the eleven members of the 'special' class and the children with Reading Ages below 9 years) had more favourable attitudes than the overall averages of the other two schools. A major strength of School **A** appears to have been the appropriateness of its history curriculum, a fundamental principle being the policy of matching and, where necessary, modifying the syllabus to meet the needs of pupils of varying abilities. Flexibility and variety were also factors behind its success. Every effort was made to organise fieldwork for low achievers and to provide suitable reading material. Thus every member of the department commented on the success of 'transport' (the development topic) because, as one teacher put it, 'We were able to use evidence which is available locally – canal trail, housing, etc.' The Head of Department attributed its success to 'the very fact that it is

Table 1.5   *Percentages of Low Achievers finding History Important and Interesting (Based on 150 Pupils in Three Secondary Schools)*

CRITERIA	SCHOOL		
	A	B	C
Importance	53	34	30
Interest	59	23	40

local and something the pupils can identify with easily.' The use of suitable reading materials was achieved without their content distorting the stated aims and objectives of the syllabus. Thus, for example, when it was found that some of the introductory units of the Schools Council History 13–16 project were too difficult for low achievers, the publications of the *Place, Time and Society* project were used instead, because they served the same purpose but had a lower level of readability.

In their efforts to meet the needs of the less able, the history curricula of Schools **B** and **C** revealed a number of serious weaknesses, including some, or all, of the following: a lack of stated aims and objectives; the inability to cope with the demands of mixed-ability teaching; the use of textbooks and other materials that were unsuitable; and the lack of audio-visual and other concrete aids to learning. However, the figures relating to School **A** are hardly encouraging. Although the survey is very limited in scale, it indicates that there is no room for complacency; history does not appear to be a popular subject with low achievers.

CONCLUSION

This chapter has been written on the strength of the premise that any study of educational provision should begin by focussing attention on the recipients; in this case pupils of low academic ability. A general understanding necessitates an examination of specific learning difficulties, stages of cognitive development, and attitudes and motivation (particularly how pupils view their own problems). A complex picture has emerged: pupils with learning difficulties cannot be regarded as a homogeneous group, and a successful curriculum must cater for individual needs.

It has been argued that there is a strong case for regarding the need for specialist educational provision in the widest possible sense: to include those pupils unable to cope with external examinations at sixteen plus. It is often lamented in schools that these pupils are fed on a watered down academic curriculum which is both inadequate and inappropriate. The whole curriculum for the child of below-average ability is in need of serious revision; and this encompasses a broader band of children than the least able ten or fifteen per cent.

REFERENCES

1 See, for example, A. A. Williams, *Basic subjects for slow learners.* Methuen, 1970; P. Bell, *Basic teaching for slow learners.* Muller, 1970; R. Gulliford, *Backwardness and educational failure.* NFER, 1969; W. Brennan, *Shaping the education of slow learners.* Routledge & Kegan Paul, 1974
2 Warnock Report, *Special educational needs.* HMSO, 1978, pp. 40–41
3 W. Brennan, *Changing special education.* Open University Press, 1982, p. 59

4 W. Brennan, *op. cit.* 1974, p. 46

5 C. McCall, 'Remedial strategies in secondary schools'. *Forum*, vol. 19, no. 2, 1977

6 J. Bruner, *The process of education*. Harvard, 1960, p. 35

7 *Ibid.*, p. 35

8 W. Brennan, *Curricular needs of slow learners*. Evans/Methuen, 1979, p. 149

9 B. Bernstein, *Class codes and controls*, 3 vols. Routledge & Kegan Paul, 1971–73

10 G. Bernbaum, 'Language and history teaching'. In W. Burston and C. Green (eds.), *Handbook for history teachers*. Methuen, 1972

11 See, for example, R. Brooks, *Bright delinquents: the story of a unique school*. NFER, 1973

12 See, for example, M. Saunders, *Class control and behaviour problems*. McGraw-Hill, 1979; D. Galloway et al, *Schools and disruptive pupils*. Longman, 1982; D. Tattum, *Disruptive pupils in schools and units*. John Wiley, 1982; K. Topping, *Educational systems for disruptive adolescents*. Calderdale, 1983

13 W. Brennan, *op. cit.* 1979, p. 152

14 See, for example, J. Francis-Williams, *Children with specific learning difficulties*. Pergamon, 1974; D. Crystal, *Introduction to language pathology*. Arnold/NFER, 1980; P. Tansley and J. Panckhurst, *Children with specific learning difficulties*. NFER, 1981

15 M. D. Wilson, *Slow learners and the secondary school history curriculum*. Unpublished M.Ed. dissertation, University of Exeter, 1981

16 See, for example, C. Burt, *Mental and scholastic tests*. Staples Press, 1947

17 S. Hegarty, 'Fair play in assessment'. *Times Educational Supplement*, 13.5.1977

18 E. A. Peel, *The pupils thinking*. Oldbourne, 1960; E. A. Peel, *The nature of adolescent judgement*. Staples, 1971; E. A. Peel, 'Some problems in the psychology of history teaching' in W. Burston and D. Thompson (eds.), *Studies in the nature and teaching of history*. Routledge & Kegan Paul, 1967

19 E. A. Peel, *Adolescent thinking in relation to secondary school progress*. Lecture at the University of Exeter, 12.6.1980

20 *Ibid*

21 J. Bruner, *op. cit.* 1960, p. 9

22 W. Alexander, 'Intelligence: concrete and abstract'. Monograph 19, *British Journal of Psychology*. 1935

23 J. Duncan, *The education of the ordinary child*. Nelson, 1942

24 F. J. Schonell, *Backwardness in basic subjects*. Oliver & Boyd, 1942, p. 51

25 A. Simon and L. O. Ward, 'An evaluation of an approach to history for remedial pupils' *Remedial Education*, vol. 8, no. 1, 1973

26 M. B. Booth, 'Inductive thinking in history – the 14–16 age range' In G. Jones and L. Ward (eds.), *New history, old problems*, Swansea, 1978

27 D. G. Watts, *The learning of history*. Routledge & Kegan Paul, 1972, p. 20

28 For a useful review of the research, see N. J. Entwistle and J. D. Nisbet, *Educational research in action*. Hodder & Stoughton, 1972, pp. 153–184

29 For example, A. Simon and L. O. Ward, 'Variables influencing attitudes to history among comprehensive school pupils'. *Teaching History*, vol. IV, 1975; A. Simon and L. O. Ward, 'Variables influencing attitudes to aspects of history'. *Teaching History*, vol. IV, 1975; M. B. Booth, 'A recent research project into children's historical thinking and its implications for history teaching' *Perspectives*, 4, 1980

30 M. D. Wilson, 'The attitudes of slow-learning adolescents to the teaching and study of history' *Teaching History*, 34, 1982; M. D. Wilson, *op. cit.* 1981, pp. 53–105

31 Schools Council, *Young School Leavers*, Enquiry no. 1 Evans/Methuen, 1968

2

Curriculum Pre-planning and Situational Analysis

INTRODUCTION

Stated aims and objectives in history syllabuses are frequently cosmetic. They are sometimes platitudinous, sometimes pedantic, but they nearly always relate more comfortably to the ideals of educational theory than to achievements in classroom practice. Of course, the perfect syllabus does not exist, and periodic reviews and alterations are inevitable. However, serious miscalculations in syllabus planning can be avoided if we take into account not only those developments which are desirable but also those which are practicable under the circumstances. Most teachers will recollect instances when schemes of work succeeded admirably with one group of pupils, only to be rejected by another group of similar age and ability, especially if in a different school. More senior members of staff will also be able to recall instances of highly successful syllabuses being introduced into other schools and suffering a kind of 'tissue rejection'. Curriculum pre-planning in the form of a situational analysis is practical management – the identification of strengths and weaknesses and the anticipation of obstacles and opportunities before embarking on a programme of curriculum development. It is a vital idiographic perspective; the syllabus must be seen to satisfy the needs of the pupils and the staff of the particular school in question.

A useful starting point is to identify the problems encountered in teaching history to pupils with learning difficulties, especially as perceived by the teachers themselves.

PROBLEM ANALYSIS: TEACHERS' PERCEPTIONS

A pilot study of teachers' attitudes was conducted in 1980 as part of a wider research project on low achievers and the history curriculum[1]. This involved analysing the responses of eighteen teachers, from four comprehensive schools, on a teacher attitude questionnaire (Appendix B); but the sample is so small that the findings can only be regarded as tentative. A detailed statistical analysis of the responses to Section 17 of the questionnaire is provided in Table 2.1. In

Table 2.1   *Teacher Problem Ratings – Pilot Study (1980)*

INDIVIDUAL SCHOOL RATING

PROBLEM	A	B	C	D	Overall Mean	Rank Order
1	5.4	2.8	5.6	5.5	4.89	7
2	5.8	3.5	4.6	6.5	5.11	5
3	4.8	5.5	6.4	5.8	5.61	2=
4	5.0	5.0	6.4	5.5	5.50	4
5	6.2	5.3	5.4	5.5	5.61	2=
6	3.2	5.5	3.8	2.8	3.78	9=
7	6.4	5.5	5.6	6.0	5.89	1
8	1.6	3.3	2.4	4.5	2.83	13
9	2.2	4.5	4.0	3.0	3.78	9=
10	2.4	4.0	1.2	5.0	3.00	12
11	5.4	4.3	4.6	4.8	4.78	8
12	3.2	3.0	2.8	4.3	3.28	11
13	5.2	4.0	5.2	5.5	5.00	6

Section 17, the teachers were asked to indicate the degree of importance attached to specific problems on an Osgood semantic differential scale ranging from 1 (minor problem) to 7 (serious problem). The staff were asked to respond in accordance with their personal experiences. The problems listed were as follows:

 1 Disruptive behaviour
 2 Absenteeism
 3 Limited pupil concentration
 4 Lack of pupil motivation
 5 Syllabus content
 6 The range of pupil ability
 7 Textbook suitability
 8 History being a compulsory subject
 9 Pupil immaturity
10 An unsupportive Remedial Department
11 Unsupportive parents
12 Timetable arrangements
13 Lack of specialised training (in coping with low achievers).

There was general agreement between the staff that the most serious problems were the unsuitability of most textbooks, the low level of pupil concentration and weaknesses in their own history syllabuses. The teachers were frank in admitting their shortcomings, especially in doubting their ability to provide courses that were appropriate to the needs of the less able pupils. The respondents did not generally regard the school timetable and liaison (or lack of it) with the Remedial Department as significant problems. Most of the teachers were satisfied with the provision of single and occasionally double periods because of their pupils' limited spans of concentration. In School **C**, liaison between the History and Remedial departments was exceptionally good, including co-operation in team-teaching, but in the other schools there was little, if any, communication between the two departments. It was surprising – not to say disturbing – to find that staff did not regard this as a significant difficulty. This confirms the view that many subject departments are still largely insular and autonomous; it also probably indicates that subject departments have limited expectations of the Remedial Department, or a narrow perspective of its role throughout the school.

Differences in teachers' ratings of problems tended to reflect differences in organisation. The most extreme contrast was the response to Problem 6 – coping with the range of pupil ability. In School **B** (with a mixed-ability system) it was regarded as the most serious of the thirteen problems; in the other schools, it came only ninth, tenth and thirteenth in rank order. In sharp contrast, the problems of absenteeism and disruptive behaviour were regarded as minimal by the staff of School **B** (ranked only tenth and thirteenth respectively) but considered far more serious problems in the other schools. Although history teachers in School **B** were dissatisfied with mixed-ability teaching, they acknowledged its social benefits for the less able, thus corroborating the sociological arguments in favour of non-streaming.

Three years later, the same questionnaire was completed by nineteen history teachers from seventeen secondary schools throughout Lincolnshire[2]. The statistical analysis of Section 17 is shown in Table 2.2. In some respects this

Table 2.2   *Teacher Problem Ratings – Lincolnshire Survey (1983)*

PROBLEM	Overall Mean	Standard Deviation	Rank Order
1	3.63	1.78	9
2	3.21	1.94	12
3	5.68	0.86	1
4	4.53	1.14	3
5	3.37	1.38	10=
6	4.63	1.98	2
7	4.32	2.08	5
8	2.95	1.76	13
9	4.47	1.57	4
10	3.37	2.01	10=
11	3.79	1.79	7
12	3.68	2.08	8
13	4.21	1.79	6

study is consistent with the first: both indicate that limited pupil concentration and lack of pupil motivation are regarded as very serious problems. However, there are some notable differences. In the Lincolnshire survey, problem 6 (the range of pupil ability) has a high ranking (the second most serious problem of the thirteen). This is in line with School **B**, but at variance with the other three schools in the original pilot study. Evidently, this problem is of widespread concern to teachers. The least consistent results relate to problems 2 (pupil absenteeism), 5 (syllabus content) and 9 (pupil immaturity). This could be partly due to difficulties of interpretation. A high pupil absence rate, for example, may be regarded as a major problem for teachers who are concerned about continuity and sequential learning. Others – more cynically perhaps – may regard the absence of the more disruptive pupils as a problem for the pastoral team and the Educational Welfare Service. For the classroom teacher, it can result in a less stressful environment with the added bonus of an improved pupil-teacher ratio: from this view-point a positive advantage rather than a problem.

Essentially, the problems encountered by the history teachers in trying to cope with low achievers fall into three main inter-related categories: problem pupils and pupils with problems; weaknesses in the curriculum; and difficulties more clearly related to aspects of organisation. Each of these can be examined in more detail.

PUPIL ANALYSIS

However useful a general knowledge of learning difficulties may be, it must be remembered that each child presents a unique set of problems. The teacher needs to compile an educational profile on each of his/her pupils as an aid to identifying initial difficulties. Information thus gained should help the teacher to plan a programme of instruction that will meet individual needs more effectively.

The use of a pupil proforma can be a useful way of assessing learning difficulties. In the example provided (Fig. 2.1) the check list is designed to draw the teacher's attention to likely problems through classroom observation. Space is provided for comment and clarification, not only on a pupil's weaknesses but also on his/her strengths and interests, for these could provide the key to motivation. As the analysis is essentially subjective, it is helpful to gain the opinions of colleagues who also teach the child. Is the child encountering problems only in history lessons, or can certain problems be identified in most subjects? Finding answers to questions such as these is a necessary step towards planning an effective strategy of remediation.

In addition to classroom observation, discussions with remedial and language specialists who teach the same children should prove very worthwhile. Reference to school records, including the reports of former teachers and educational psychologists, will alert the history teacher to a wide range of

Fig. 2.1   Pupil Profile – Learning Difficulties

Name of Pupil (use initials or code)......................................

Sex of Pupil ....

Please tick only those descriptions which on the whole describe the above pupil when you teach him/her. This is a profile based on CLASSROOM OBSERVATION.

1 Problems with reading	☐	14 Very limited vocabulary	☐
2 Problems with writing	☐	15 Very limited general knowledge	☐
3 Avoids work	☐	16 Lacks concentration	☐
4 Seeks routine tasks	☐	17 Rarely joins in discussions	☐
5 Slow to carry out tasks	☐	18 Hyperactive/irritable	☐
6 Rarely finishes work	☐	19 Tired/lethargic	☐
7 Finishes work too quickly	☐	20 Unable to follow simple instructions	☐
8 Loses/forgets equipment	☐	21 Difficulty with hearing	☐
9 Seeks attention	☐	22 Difficulty in seeing blackboard	☐
10 Avoids attention	☐	23 Has speech impediment	☐
13 Clumsy in practical work	☐	24 Aggressive behaviour	☐
12 Skips lessons	☐	25 Disruptive behaviour	☐
13 Often late to lessons	☐	26 Dreamy/withdrawn	☐

Additional comments/observations...

....

....

....

....

Apparent strengths/interests...

....

....

....

....

Signed...........   Date........

problems. School records are almost certain to include the data from various standardised tests. These vary in their usefulness, but one of the most helpful and comprehensive is the series of Richmond tests of basic skills[3]. This comprises eleven tests, covering: vocabulary; reading comprehension; three language tests (usage, spelling, capital letters); two mathematics tests (concepts, problem-solving); and three tests on work study skills (map reading, graphs and tables; and knowledge and use of reference materials). Comparing a child's test results can be very illuminating. Pronounced failure in one or two tests may be symptomatic of specific learning disabilities (e.g. perceptual disorders in the case of poor readers of good general ability), or educational deficiencies at the primary level (e.g. a very limited vocabulary or lack of work study skills, which could be a reflection of what the child has not been taught). On the basis of these tests, it is possible to make comparisons between the educational performance of children from the different feeder primary schools. However, it must be remembered that differences in pupil attainment not only reflect the measure of a school's success but also variations in the social composition of catchment areas, particularly in the case of neighbourhood schools.

More specifically, history teachers also need to be able to assess a child's aptitude for the study of their subject. Where there is continuity of staffing and close liaison between members of the department, formal procedures for this may prove unnecessary; but the transition from primary to secondary school usually marks a significant discontinuity. According to a recent HMI report:

> There would appear to be an urgent need to establish middle or primary school liaison with regard to history. Few secondary schools seem to be clear about the details of history courses in their feeder schools and there appears to be a considerable amount of overlap and consequent wasted effort.[4]

It follows, therefore, that some form of subject 'pre-testing' on transition to the secondary school would serve a useful purpose in gauging each pupil's initial level of attainment. The following may be regarded as essential components of a history pre-test:

1 *Factual Knowledge* – The pupils can be presented with a check list of key words and names associated with the proposed topic or course of study. They can be asked to tick those which they know something about and to mark by a cross those which are unfamiliar. Finally, they can be asked to comment on three or four of the most familiar items. The teacher's assessment will reveal gaps in the pupils' knowledge along with any misconceptions indicated in the written statements.

2 *Conceptual Knowledge* – Pupils will need to be able to see meaningful relationships between groups of words and phrases as a basis for understanding. Two simple examples are given below:
A. Roads, canals and railways are all forms of ....
B. Swords, guns and tanks are all types of ....

3 *Skills* – There is a very wide range of skills which are regarded as essential to

the study of history; and it is to be expected that most of these will have to be introduced and developed throughout the course of the child's secondary education. However, at pre-test level, the history teacher will need to assess the pupil's competence in basic reference skills, reading and writing, chronology and numeracy, and understanding of maps.

4 *Interests* – Awareness of pupil interests can provide clues to improving motivation by linking these, where possible, to the history curriculum. Children's reading habits and interests are a useful index[5]. In a recent study of low achievers, over ninety per cent of the pupils said that they enjoyed some reading for pleasure, particularly comics and stories of horror, adventure, mystery and romance[6]. Such themes fire the imagination and develop an empathetic response to human situations; and they are to be found in large measure in the study of history. A summary of the reading interests of 150 low achievers is shown in Table 2.3.

Table 2.3   *The Reading Interests of 150 Low Achievers*

READING MATERIAL	Col. 1	Col. 2
Books: horror/mystery/adventure	21.0	1
Comics	20.2	2
Romance magazines	16.4	3
Daily newspapers	8.4	4
Books: sport/hobbies	8.0	5
Books: cars/motor bikes	6.3	6
Pop music magazines	5.4	7 =
Books: animals/nature	5.4	7 =
Miscellaneous	8.9	

Column 1: Percentage of overall responses
Column 2: Rank order of popularity

CURRICULUM REVIEW AND ANALYSIS

Teachers' doubts about the suitability of their courses for low achievers were confirmed by two major reports published in 1979. The School Council enquiry into the curricular needs of slow learners surveyed 502 primary, secondary and special schools, concluding that the proportion of successful curricula was in the region of only fifty per cent. The inadequacy of the history curriculum, along with other humanities subjects, reflected not only the language difficulties of low achievers but also the low level of success of language teaching in the schools surveyed[7]. The HMI report on secondary education, based on a study of school 'provision' and pupil 'response', confirmed this pessimism. Four serious problems were highlighted: a lack of coherence in the curriculum as a whole; schemes of work rarely being pitched at a level 'which both retained interest and demanded worthwhile achievement'; a lack of specialist remedial provision for pupils in their last two years at school; and very few teachers having the necessary combination of skills in both remedial education and a specialist subject[8].

A root cause of these difficulties has been 'curriculum distancing' – the separation of the remedial curriculum from the mainstream. In some schools the divisions are obvious, for example when low achievers are taught in separate buildings and follow a substantially different timetable under the aegis of specialist remedial teachers. However, the dichotomy is also evident in more subtle ways. For obvious reasons, remedial specialists are very child-centred in their approach, concentrating their efforts on aspects of educational psychology (appertaining to learning difficulties) and the teaching of fundamental skills. On the other hand, the subject specialists tend to be more academically orientated. Teaching bright pupils is generally regarded as more satisfying because the pupils are better motivated and are more likely to achieve examination success – tangible reinforcements for the teacher. I remember so vividly one Head of Department giving vent to her frustrations when she cried: 'Teaching those boys (low achievers in their fifth year) is so depressing; I feel no more than an extension of the Special Needs Department.' But the frustration arises more from an inability to cope successfully with the less able than from a feeling of apathy towards their needs. In the words of L. O. Ward: 'Very few historians possess the knowledge and experience of slow-learning children to enable them to analyse what is distinctive about their subject which might, in some form, usefully contribute to the curriculum for the less able child.'[9] This unfortunate gulf is reflected both in styles of teaching and the nature and suitability of reading materials. More will be said about these issues in later chapters.

The failure of the history curriculum to cater for special educational needs is apparent from a review of curriculum development and innovation. When Mary Price wrote her influential article, which saw 'a real danger of history disappearing from the timetable as a subject in its own right'[10], the history specialists responded to the threats and criticisms with something of a crusading spirit. The wave of reforms in historical education, known popularly as the 'New History', promoted family, oral and local history, the use of games and simulations and primary sources, the encouragement of an objectives approach in syllabus planning, and the creation of the Schools Council's widely implemented *History 13–16 Project*. But in all this spate of activity there was virtually nothing done with low achievers specifically in mind. Gosden and Sylvester produced a publication in 1968 which arose out of evening sessions on teaching history to pupils of average and below-average ability, organised by the University of Leeds Institute of Education in 1967[11]. The authors raised some important questions, but their focus of attention was very much on the average, rather than the below-average, child. The follow-up was disappointing. None of the major general texts on the teaching of history contained anything of substance on low achievers[12], and all that seemed at hand was a small number of short articles written from the remedial end of the spectrum. They served a useful function in breaking ice and drawing attention to a serious deficiency[13].

In some ways, the year 1978 marked a turning-point. Not only was the Warnock Report published with its far-reaching recommendations[14], but a conference was held by the Historical Association which drew attention to the problems of teaching history to young and less academic pupils. Among its recommendations were: a change in the bias of the journal *Teaching History* from educational theory to more practical issues; a greater effort to produce suitable materials for teachers of the less able, including a course book written jointly by a historian and a reading specialist; more research into the use of language and history teaching; and a rational justification, expressed in terms of aims and specific objectives, for the teaching of history to pupils of all ages and abilities.

Since these recommendations were made, progress has undoubtedly been achieved[15]. General works on remedial education have drawn more attention to the teaching of specialist subjects, including some with sections or chapters on history[16]; the Historical Association commissioned Evelyn Cowie to write the pamphlet *History and the Slow-Learning Child* (1979); and several articles on history teaching and the less able have appeared in the journal *Teaching History* since 1980. Course texts and other curricular materials, which teachers should find of great value, have also been published in recent years[17]. Two excellent and practical handbooks deserve a special mention: *Curriculum Ideas – Catering for the Slow Learner: History* (New South Wales Department of Education, 1981) and *Teaching History to Slow-learning Children in Secondary Schools*, edited by V. McIver (Department of Education, Northern Ireland, 1982). Both examine the theoretical background as well as suggesting specific classroom strategies. Although the latter is geared to the needs of schools in Northern Ireland, the principles will be helpful to all history teachers. The Australian project extols the virtues of the structured learning approach through behavioural objectives, but is consequently fairly rigid and prescriptive in its recommendations. As useful as these recent initiatives are, a great deal remains to be done, both in terms of research and in the publication of classroom materials.

History teachers would be well advised to review their current practice and syllabus content in the light of these recent developments. An honest reappraisal which seeks to identify strengths and weaknesses may hold the key to future success. Open discussion at meetings, the sharing of ideas and expertise, and consultation regarding proposed changes are all conducive to staff harmony and professional advancement within the department. Above all, subject teachers must have a sense of commitment and responsibility towards the needs of the less able. In the words of Charles Gains: 'Remedial education is not a subject, although it is often treated thus, but a horizontal concept involving all teachers to some degree.'[18]

ORGANISATIONAL ANALYSIS 1: CLASSROOM MANAGEMENT AND PUPIL MOTIVATION

Good classroom management is essential to the creation of a milieu that is conducive to effective learning. Some useful suggestions, especially for the inexperienced teacher, have been published[19]. The main recommendations can be subsumed under the following headings:

1 *Standards* – These must be made explicit to the pupils from the outset, and should include such matters as presentation of work, punctuality, courtesy, classroom tidiness and procedures for the distribution and return of equipment. The pupils should know where they stand.

2 *Consistency* – Once the standards of discipline have been established they can only be maintained through a consistency of approach; when pupils know what to expect they have a greater sense of security. One difficulty likely to arise is the inconsistency of expectation between different members of staff who teach the same group. There can be no easy solution to this problem, except to urge closer liaison between teachers and departments. The Remedial or Special Needs Department can act in an advisory capacity.

3 *Preparedness* – Teachers should anticipate possible causes of trouble and take preventive measures. They would be well advised to keep a 'survival kit' of spare pens and pencils and any other basic equipment, and to give careful consideration to pupil seating arrangements. How the children are seated will determine, to a large extent, the success of the pedagogical approach – formal or informal. Teachers should also avoid seating children near potential allies in trouble.

4 *Flexibility* – Although meticulous planning and preparation are to be recommended, the teacher's approach needs to be sufficiently flexible to cater for individual needs. Work must always be ready for the child who completes the assignment ahead of time, as idleness breeds frustration and mischief. When a lesson fails miserably, it is vital to become introspective and to analyse what went wrong. The 'one-off' situation may well be the result of extraneous circumstances, but persistent difficulties are more likely to result from inappropriate schemes of work. Teachers must evaluate what they are doing and be willing to change course if necessary. There is no disgrace in seeking advice; it is something we must all do from time to time.

Pupil motivation depends on more than a clinical efficiency in classroom management. Professor A. H. Maslow, for example, has argued that human motivation involves at least five basic needs[20]:

1 Physiological well-being – nourishment, rest, comfort
2 Safety – the avoidance of inconsistency, fears, humiliation and injustice
3 Love – affection and a sense of belonging
4 Esteem – self-respect, recognition, hope, achievement and independence
5 Self-actualisation – the desire to realise one's own potential.

The fact that many low achievers are socially disadvantaged and have had a protracted history of failure at school is clear indication that a 'needs-based' theory of learning has considerable potency. Emphasis should be on reward and reinforcement for a child's achievements and efforts[21].

Research in the USA has shown that pupil performance is significantly related to teachers' attitudes – in particular their sense of 'efficacy', that is to say, 'the extent to which teachers believe that they have the capacity to affect student performance.'[22] In two Rand Corporation evaluation studies, teachers' sense of efficacy was measured from their degree of agreement/disagreement (on a five-point Likert scale) to the following statements:

1 When it comes right down to it, a teacher really can't do much because most of a student's motivation and performance depends on his or her home environment.
2 If I really try hard, I can get through to even the most difficult or unmotivated students.

It was found that teachers' sense of efficacy was significantly related to pupils' achievement in high school basic skills classes; and it was also related to the maintenance of a warm, accepting classroom climate. Moreover,

> Teachers with high efficacy attitudes were more likely to maintain high academic standards, concentrate on academic instruction, monitor students' on-task behaviour, and work to build friendly, non-threatening relationships with their low-achieving students than were teachers with low efficacy attitudes.[23]

Conversely, teachers with low efficacy attitudes tended to use harsh control tactics; to stratify their pupils according to ability; and to give preferential treatment to their most able students.[24] However, certain conditions in the schools militated against high efficacy attitudes, including isolation, uncertainty, powerlessness, and the lack of economic rewards and social recognition.

ORGANISATIONAL ANALYSIS 2: THE TIMETABLE

The timetable is an 'enabling device' in the sense that it is a means of implementing stated curricular aims and objectives:

> A timetable, above all, is not to be seen as a problem but as a vehicle for extending opportunities to teachers to incorporate what they will into their teaching method and content.[25]

A number of constraints must be taken into account:

1 *Pupil–Teacher Ratio* – A generous allowance is to be recommended for remedial groups; usually a ratio of about 1 : 15. However, this is likely to cause larger classes elsewhere, and may also conflict with the desire to sustain minority options in the fourth, fifth and sixth forms – a conflict exacerbated

by the current climate of contraction and falling rolls. The integration of some courses and the integration of low achievers into the mainstream curriculum may ease some of these problems; but proposals such as these should be justified on educational grounds and not implemented simply as administrative expedients.

2 *Resource Allocation* – A progressive history curriculum which relies on the use of audio-visual aids and other specialist equipment will require timetable allocation to.specialist rooms because of the difficulties in transporting the equipment.

3 *Time Allocation* – This is likely to be considerably limited, as most schools are likely to hold the view that pupils with learning difficulties are to be best served by following a curriculum largely devoted to the mastery of basic skills and concepts that are essential preparation for adult and working life, including basic skills in literacy and numeracy, social/life skills, and practical/vocational skills. History, therefore, is often allocated no more than a couple of single periods a week. Many teachers are satisfied with this arrangement because their pupils allegedly have limited spans of concentration, but more practical activities such as field-work will require double periods or even blocked time. Again it must be stated that one way of achieving this is through subject integration. A single field course, for example, can combine elements of history and geography, as well as encourage inter-departmental co-operation and cross-fertilisation of ideas.

Timetabling also requires vision and sensitivity in the allocation of staff to forms. The comments of a history teacher in my Lincolnshire survey show great insight and make the point forcibly:

> I find the present group (of low achievers) in Year Three very amenable and keen, the vast majority working to capacity. In the previous year, the group was very diverse, extremely difficult to motivate, although the basic educational problems were very similar. The present Third Year class I took for History and French in Year Two. In Year Three, I have them for two periods of History, three periods of French, and I am also their Form Teacher. Taking them such a lot from their entry to school has resulted in a good general relationship with the group. By Year Three I know their strengths and weaknesses, and they know my expectations regarding work and acceptable class behaviour. I feel that perhaps the level of familiarity has a lot to do with the continuity of time spent with this group. Colleagues who have had this set comparatively infrequently experience great problems. . . . Perhaps a group of five or six staff working with them for the equivalent of one day a week may provide just enough continuity, but also just enough variety.

Low achievers need a secure and stable learning environment, in which they are taught by staff who have had the opportunity of building a good relationship with them over a period of time: stability arises from continuity and consistency of approach.

There is evidence to suggest that timetabling arrangements make the needs of the more able external examination candidates a clear priority, and this is unlikely to change while there is talk of holding schools accountable on the strength of published examination results. Moreover, it is possible that many department heads, in coping with the demands of teaching external examination courses, are unable to find time to implement as many curricular changes as they would like for the less able and younger pupils. Dr Stephen Ball's perceptive study of Beachside Comprehensive exemplifies the implications of the 'pressured academic environment.' In his analysis of eight academic departments (including history) he found that approximately forty per cent of O- and A-level teaching was retained by heads of departments. He concluded that 'the most experienced teachers spend most of their time teaching the most able pupils', and that 'the"others" are responsible for three-quarters of the CSE and band 3 and remedial lessons.'[26] If this is typical of history departments in other comprehensives – and further research will have to substantiate this – then there is clear cause for concern if we are to accept Roger Moore's claim that history should be 'of vital importance and interest to all children and not just an academically orientated handful.'[27] Indeed, if we fall short of this ideal then history could only be justified as an *option* for an academic elite, and its place in a core curriculum would be placed in jeopardy.[28]

Finally, mention should be made of timetabling as a device for ensuring the optimal deployment of remedial and subject teachers, particularly with regard to initiatives such as team-teaching. Successful experiments in team-teaching have certainly been reported, including Fearn's study of the scheme implemented by the Remedial and History departments at Westfield Comprehensive in Derbyshire. The main advantages of the system over separate provision for the less able were as follows:

1 The problems of isolation and lack of co-ordination between the two departments were overcome. The skills of the remedial and history teachers were combined for the benefit of the children, the history teachers preparing the lessons, the remedial teachers assuming charge of the lessons and advising on the preparation of materials. Thus the teachers were able to learn from each other, not only in the actual teaching but also in the preparation.
2 Closer supervision was possible with two members of staff present – a clear advantage for the low achievers, who could be given individual help from one teacher, while the other supervised the whole class.
3 Larger teaching groups led to the more frequent use of audio-visual aids, which were no longer 'an occasional luxury'.
4 The oral element of the lessons was more stimulating with two teachers present: 'It was easier to persuade pupils to make an active contribution when both teachers engaged in discussion than it was when just one was speaking.'[29]

However, experiments of this kind should be implemented with caution. Success will depend on the willingness of the staff to co-operate and learn from each other. As David Trethowan pointed out in a recent article, breaking down barriers is not always easy:

> Staff do not expect to have their work examined, to be observed while working, or to have targets set. There has been a long tradition among teachers that it is unprofessional to expect to be watched in action with a class. . . [30]

Furthermore, the use of a remedial specialist in a team-teaching situation is almost certain to limit the time available for specialist withdrawal work:

> Helping the subject specialist to ask better questions, provide more attractive materials or get round the whole class so that everyone's written work is seen before the end of the lesson is a helpful contribution which makes for better teaching. But it is still necessary to question whether improving the quality of teaching for all children is the most effective way of providing extra help for children with learning difficulties.[31]

It would be unwise to be too prescriptive: schools must choose organisational structures which best suit their particular needs and which make the most effective use of the staff and resources available to them.

ORGANISATIONAL ANALYSIS 3: MIXED-ABILITY TEACHING

It has already been noted earlier in this chapter that coping with the range of pupil ability is of widespread concern to teachers, particularly in a mixed-ability situation. It is therefore necessary to question whether or not integration of this kind is the most appropriate way to teach history to children of low academic achievement.

There is certainly recent research evidence to suggest that mixed-ability teaching works to the advantage of pupils, including low achievers. It was concluded, for example, that the experiment of integrating remedial pupils at Llanishen High School (allowing for some withdrawal periods) led to the following benefits:

> Pupils are now much better behaved when in the vicinity of classrooms. They appear more willing to accept help from their peers and teachers, to work co-operatively in groups and often show a real desire to help others who are more able or less able than they are. In the groups studied it was found that reading, spelling and arithmetic skills improved more significantly under the integrated new organisation than in the old segregated special class type of organisation. Consequently many more remedial pupils are now being returned to full-time work in regular classes. . . [32]

Successful mixed-ability teaching has also been reported with specific reference to the teaching of history. The key to the success, apart from the firm conviction on the part of the staff that the system really works, seems to have been the use of team-teaching (involving the close co-operation between remedial and subject teachers in the classroom) and the build-up of adequate resources to facilitate individualised schemes of work, such as graded worksheets[33]. However, we have already raised a number of questions about the efficacy of team-teaching, and a recent DES report criticised the over-emphasis on individualised learning. Speaking of mixed-ability teaching in history lessons, the following observations were made:

> The biggest single weakness is the unexamined assumption that mixed-ability teaching means individualised learning based on worksheets. More often than not these simply offer opportunities for pupils of different abilities to work at different rates. Skills are limited to the collection, memorising, and regurgitation of knowledge. . . . Good practice. . . recognises that a reliance on work and assignment sheets threatens group and classwork and may cause the learning of history to be associated with tedious, isolated and lonely tasks.[34]

The Schools Council working party into the curricular needs of slow learners also expressed concern about the progress of low achievers in mixed-ability groups, concluding that 'the curriculum (and indeed teaching) for slow learners tends to be more successful in situations where there is a degree of segregation which ensures that the problem presented by slow learners is recognised, defined and followed through.'[35]

On the strength of available evidence, the debate on segregation versus mixed-ability teaching remains inconclusive. The success or failure of the latter would appear to depend on a highly complex set of circumstances. It is for this reason that the 'pointers' for good future practice, outlined by the most recent full-scale investigation into mixed-ability teaching conducted by the NFER, concentrate on identifying those contexts which either facilitate or constrain mixed-ability teaching.[36] Important considerations include the following:

1 *Management* – Innovation on the lines of mixed-ability teaching was more likely to succeed when teachers were consulted and persuaded to support such changes.
2 *Teacher support* – It is clear that teachers need special help in coping with mixed-ability classes, including adequate provision for resource-based learning, in-service training (where necessary), and a favourable pupil – teacher ratio (the possibility of using peer tutors and paraprofessionals has been recommended by some researchers).
3 *The ages of pupils* – Mixed-ability teaching was generally regarded as more appropriate for younger pupils because of a number of serious constraints in the teaching of older children – particularly the growing pressures of preparing students for external examinations.
4 *The nature of the subject discipline* – It is generally agreed among teachers that some subjects are more appropriate than others for mixed-ability groups. The least appropriate, including mathematics and modern languages, are disciplines characterised by a sequential structure, the need for highly specific pupil responses, complex/abstract concepts, and a highly technical vocabulary.

How far history teachers regard their discipline as appropriate to the needs of mixed-ability teaching is far from certain:

> The teachers who saw problems in teaching history to mixed-ability classes were
> concerned over basic reading skills and conceptual development linked with the
> pupils' understanding of vocabulary. 'History must involve reading' contrasted
> with the 'changing resources and methods – Jackdaws, films, slides' approach
> adopted by teachers who did consider the subject as suited to a mixed ability
> approach.[37]

The 'history must involve reading' approach has been criticised for its excessive
reliance on individual learning, especially the over-use of graded worksheets;
but are the more progressive teaching methods, alluded to above, any more
successful in a mixed-ability setting? A recent research project conducted by Dr
Martin Booth provides some useful answers to this question[38].

Dr Booth's project was a detailed study of mixed-ability teaching in a first-
year integrated humanities course (with a strong historical component) at
Swanley comprehensive school in Kent. The emphasis throughout the course
was on the use of evidence, the development of key concepts and pupil
involvement – particularly in developing oral skills and self-confidence through
discussions in small groups, drama and role-play. All these activities were
backed up with the use of tape recorders and other audio-visual aids. Both at
the beginning of the course (September 1980) and at the end (July 1981), the
pupils were tested for general intelligence; conceptual understanding (twenty
key concepts were selected); skills (ranging from simple comprehension to
awareness of evidence and inferential/imaginative responses); and attitudes
(based on a Likert scale). The pupils made significant gains in their intelligence
scores, their conceptual development and their skills in oral communication;
but their progress in reading and the use of written language was disappointing.
Written answers, both from the more able and less able pupils, were
unimaginative and concrete – in contrast to the lively hypothesising and
imaginative oral responses evoked during group discussions. This clearly
reflected the emphasis in teaching style.

The conclusions that can be drawn are clear. If we are to develop the widest
possible range of skills and concepts in pupils in mixed-ability settings, then an
equally wide range of teaching strategies and pupil activities must be
encouraged. There is most certainly an important place for whole class teaching
and group work, emphasising oral skills and the development of understanding
through inter-personal relationships and audio-visual aids. However, history
teachers must also endeavour to improve the reading and writing skills of their
pupils, for these are essential tools for any historical enquiry. Work of this kind
must be graded and individualised if it is to stretch the gifted child, while at the
same time catering for the needs of the low achiever.

It is important that teachers do not lose sight of the vital perspective that the
organisational framework of a school is no more than a means of facilitating the
school's instructional framework. Progress in one demands progress in the
other. In the words of Colin McCall:

> May be for too long we have sought to answer the problem of the child deemed
> 'remedial' by considering patterns of organisation rather than instructional

flexibility. Remedial classes, withdrawal systems, mixed-ability teaching situations are only as productive as the quality of the teaching method within.[39]

CONCLUSION

This chapter has inevitably been wide and diffuse in its coverage, drawing attention to a number of factors which are likely to have a significant influence on the successful implementation of a history curriculum for low achievers. If syllabus aims and objectives are to be realistic and practicable, such constraints must be taken into account. A situational analysis – in the widest possible sense – is a necessary prerequisite to good planning.

REFERENCES

1 M. D. Wilson, Slow learners and the secondary school history curriculum. Unpublished M. Ed. dissertation, University of Exeter, 1981
2 I am grateful to Mr Ray Acton, History Inspector for Lincolnshire, and the teachers who attended the in-service course at Horncastle College (March, 1983) for completing and forwarding the questionnaires
3 A. N. Hieronymus and E. F. Lindquist, *Richmond tests of basic skills, levels* 1–6 Nelson/NFER, 1982 ed.
4 DES, *History in some secondary schools in Hampshire.* HMSO, 1983
5 See, for example, F. J. Schonell, *Backwardness in basic subjects.* Oliver & Boyd, 1942, p. 115; G. M. Blair, *Diagnostic and remedial teaching.* Macmillan, 1956
6 M. D. Wilson, *op. cit.,* pp. 94–95
7 W. Brennan, *Curricular needs of slow learners.* Evans/Methuen, 1979
8 DES *Aspects of secondary Education* HMSO, 1979, Chap. 13
9 L. O. Ward, 'History for the slow learner'. *Remedial Education,* vol. 9, no. 1, 1973
10 M. Price, 'History in Danger'. *History,* vol. LIII, p. 342
11 P. Gosden and D. Sylvester, *History for the average child.* Basil Blackwell, 1968
12 See, for example, W. Burston and C. Green (eds.), *Handbook for history teachers.* Methuen, 1972; J. Chaffer and L. Taylor, *History and the history teacher.* Unwin, 1975; I. Steele (ed.), *Developments in history teaching.* Open Books, 1976
13 L. O. Ward, *op. cit.*; M. Roberts, 'History – a waste of time?'. *Special Education,* vol. 61, no. 4, 1972; N. Tate, 'How can we recreate the past?'. *Special Education,* vol. 6, no. 3, 1979
14 Warnock Report, *Special educational needs.* HMSO, 1978
15 For a useful summary of these developments, see R. McMinn, 'A feast or famine? History for slow-learning children in Northern Ireland'. *Teaching History,* 36, 1983
16 See, for example, M. Hinson (ed.), *Encouraging results.* Macdonald, 1978; D. Griffin, *Slow learners: a break in the circle.* Woburn, 1978; M. Hinson and M. Hughes (eds.), *Planning effective progress.* Hulton, 1982
17 For a comprehensive list, see V. McIver (ed.), *Teaching history to slow-learning children in secondary schools.* Belfast, 1982
18 C. W. Gains, 'Remedial education across the basic curriculum'. *Times Educational Supplement,* 26.9.1980

19 For example, V. McIver, *op. cit.*; C. Hannam et al, *The first year of teaching*. Penguin, 1976
20 A. H. Maslow, *Motivation and personality*. Harper & Row, 1954
21 I. M. Hulicka, 'The socially unmotivated'. In J. S. Roucek (ed.), *The slow learners*. Peter Owen, 1970
22 P. Ashton and R. Webb, A study of teachers' sense of efficacy. Typescript abstract, undated
23 *Ibid*
24 *Ibid*
25 DES, *Curriculum 11–16*. HMSO, 1977, p. 87
26 S. Ball, *Beachside Comprehensive: a case study of secondary schooling*. Cambridge University Press, 1981, pp. 18–19
27 R. Moore, 'History abandoned? The need for a continuing debate'. *Teaching History*, 32, 1982
28 M. D. Wilson, 'A critical view of the compulsory history curriculum 11–14'. *Teaching History*, 36, 1983.
29 E. Fearn, 'Team-teaching with the remedial stream'. *Forward Trends*, vol. 12, no. 3, 1968, pp. 97–98
30 D. Trethowan, 'Managing to learn'. *Times Educational Supplement*, 15.11.1983
31 N. Ferguson and M. Adams, 'Assessing the advantages of team teaching in remedial education: The remedial teacher's role'. *Remedial Education*, vol. 17, no. 1, 1982
32 A. C. Capron, A. Simon and L. O. Ward, 'Principles for the integration of remedial pupils in the comprehensive school'. *Remedial Education*, vol. 18, no. 2, 1983
33 J. Hull, 'Mixed ability history: a graded worksheet approach'. *Teaching History*, 22, 1978; B. L. Cooke, 'Teaching history in mixed-ability groups'. In E. C. Wragg (ed.), *Teaching mixed ability groups*. David & Charles, 1976
34 DES, *Mixed ability work in comprehensive schools*. HMSO, 1978, pp. 107–109
35 W. Brennan, *op. cit.*, 1979, pp. 18, 65, 93
36 M. Reid et al, *Mixed ability teaching: problems and possibilities*. NFER, 1981
37 *Ibid.*, p. 116
38 M. B. Booth, Mixed-ability teaching in humanities in the first year of a comprehensive school. Lecture given to the Norfolk History Teachers' Association on the 14.9.1983. On the value of practical work in mixed-ability teaching, see also A. Reid, 'Archaeology in the cause of mixed ability history'. *Teaching History*, 32, 1982
39 C. McCall, 'Remedial strategies in secondary schools'. *Forum*, vol. 19, no. 2, 1977

3
Curriculum Planning: Aims and Objectives

INTRODUCTION

'Aims' may be regarded as learning and teaching goals expressed in a very general way. They are a necessary starting point – an expression of the educational ideals we hope to attain – but their relatively imprecise and philosophical nature means that they are insufficient in themselves. 'Objectives', on the other hand, are more specific statements of purpose: the priority teaching and pupil learning intentions. They are akin to the detailed lesson plan and should provide the following information:

1 The choice of teaching methods and techniques of classroom management
2 The choice of activities and learning experiences for the children
3 The selection of learning resources
4 The time allocated to each activity, ensuring balance and a sense of pace
5 The knowledge, skills and concepts that the children are expected to have acquired as a result of their learning experiences.

The purpose of this chapter will be to examine the aims and objectives of teaching history to low achievers in some detail and to consider their implications for syllabus content. First, however, we need to take a wider perspective by considering the place of history in the context of the whole curriculum.

HISTORY IN THE CONTEXT OF THE WHOLE CURRICULUM

Few teachers would go along with Professor G. R. Elton in doubting the wisdom of teaching history to school-children[1]; but serious doubts have been expressed about the wisdom of teaching the more traditional academic subjects, including history, to children of low ability. As we have seen, there has been substantial research evidence to suggest that curricular provision for low achievers is one of the least successful aspects of secondary education. The Government has drawn attention to the problems of under-achievement and disaffection in many state schools. One of its more recent proposals is the highly publicised pilot scheme, the new Technical and Vocational Education Initiative (TVEI), which aims at dividing the school population into academic and vocational and thereby providing an education that is more suited to particular interests and aptitudes.

Of course, there is nothing new in the notion of an alternative curriculum for the less able. One of the most powerful advocates of the so-called dual curriculum is Professor G. H. Bantock. In various publications[2] he argues that the majority of pupils are ill-served by a 'watered down academic education we still provide in the core curriculum.' In place of this, he proposes a curriculum appropriate to the needs of the 'folk culture', characterised by an extension of practicality (including the study of life skills) and an emphasis on the affective – artistic (rather than the cognitive – intellectual), including aspects of contemporary popular culture and work in movement, music, art and craft. The 'fundamental discipline', he argues, should not be reading – although this should not be neglected – but the 'art of movement with its emphasis on motor skills, communal participation and opportunity to develop perception and empathy.' History has no place in Bantock's alternative curriculum.

There is much in Bantock's thesis which is consistent with the thinking of many teachers of low achievers. He rightly draws attention to the fact that many children are 'grossly and palpably under-functioning'; he rightly questions a curriculum with a narrow cognitive–intellectual base; and his emphasis on work with a practical application is consistent with what has been said about 'concrete intelligence' and the intellectual functioning of many low achievers. However, Bantock's argument raises more problems and objections than it claims to solve. Suggestions such as his, to quote Mary Warnock, 'seem to arise from a kind of despair at the actual failure of current educational practice, rather than from any serious theoretical considerations.'[3] The main criticism of the dual curriculum is the problem of selection and allocation, with all the sinister implications of inequality of educational opportunity, especially when some pupils would be nurtured on a curriculum with a greatly diminished cognitive component. In the words of Professor P. H. Hirst:

> If the acquisition of certain fundamental elements of knowledge is necessary to the achievement of the rational mind in some particular respect, then these at any rate cannot be but universal objectives for the curriculum. If the objectives of our education differ from sections of our society so as to ignore any of these elements for some of our pupils, either because they are considered too difficult, or for some reason they are thought less important for these pupils, then we are denying to them certain basic ways of rational development and we have indeed got inequality of educational opportunity of the most far-reaching kind.[4]

To speak of 'fundamental elements of knowledge' or 'basic and essential learnings'[5] is to speak of a common curriculum. Although we have not reached total agreement as to what should constitute the common core[6], it is doubtful if anyone would question the place of the humanities as an essential component. It is also generally accepted that an historical perspective is both unique and vitally important to a proper understanding of society. As David Hargreaves points out, the study of history is not necessarily any less valid if it is part of an integrated studies programme:

> An adequate understanding of one's own community and social condition does indeed require the most careful study of how the community came to be as it is. History is neeeded for that task, but it does not have to be any less disciplined just because its point of departure is an understanding of the present or because it is being undertaken in concert with (say) geographical and economic perspectives. Indeed it may well be that integrated studies will stimulate in pupils a recognition of the need for, and the point of, the disciplined study of the single-subject specialization.[7]

A core curriculum of 'basic and essential learnings' is surely necessary for all pupils, but a common curriculum should not obscure special educational needs, whether we are talking of the gifted or the slow-learning child. Hirst is himself aware that a major problem is our inexperience in designing courses that 'all pupils can take successfully', but claims that there are 'no adequate grounds for saying this is impossible when we have in fact spent so little of our effort in trying to achieve this.'[8] In ensuring adequate provision for low achievers in a core curriculum, a number of points need to be emphasised. First, it must be stressed that the common core curriculum is not the whole curriculum. Once the basic requirements have been met, flexibility can operate through an options system. Gifted children, for example, may be able to take an additional foreign language, whereas low achievers may be able to pursue additional courses of a practical or vocational nature. Secondly, within the core itself (which should include an historical component) subjects should be adapted to meet the needs of the less able. The defeatist who argues that history is too difficult for low achievers has either failed to grasp this point, or has expectations of his or her subject and pupils which are unrealistic. This point can be further clarified through reference to the work of Wilfred Brennan. He distinguishes two learning continua: skills (measured along an axis ranging from familiarity to mastery) and concepts (measured along an axis ranging from awareness to understanding). Although 'mastery' and 'understanding' are ideal target objectives, the ideal is unlikely to be fully attained except for the complete mastery of basic skills and understanding of basic concepts. However, as Brennan says: 'Slow learners need to be *aware* of many things they may not fully understand but which have a central importance in ensuring that pupils are able to relate efficiently to their natural and social environments.'[9] In achieving such an objective, Brennan argues that an awareness of the ideas of history seems essential:

> It is doubtful if any person can be socially competent without some ability to weigh the objectivity of evidence, without some knowledge of development in the affairs and institutions of men, and without some knowledge of the interdependence of people in different parts of the world and in different cultures.[10]

A full justification for the teaching of history to less able children can be appreciated from a more detailed discussion of aims and objectives.

ESTABLISHING AIMS:
THE COGNITIVE–INTELLECTUAL

According to Hirst, a fundamental aim in teaching any subject should be the development of a 'rational mind', that is to say, the development of basic concepts, the awareness of essential facts and truths, the mastery of logical operations and principles, and the application of criteria to judgements[11]. In this respect, the work of Jerome Bruner has been particularly influential. The pupil, he claims, should be concerned with learning 'the structures of subjects': their characteristic concepts, skills and modes of enquiry – what he terms their 'basic ideas', which build the foundations of the curriculum. In calling for a co-operative effort between educationists and subject specialists in drawing up such a structured approach suitable to the needs of children, Bruner is arguing for more than a full understanding of child psychology. He is calling also for 'a detailed epistemological analysis of whatever subject is in question so that its essential features may be exposed and made the basis of what is to be learned.'[12] This maxim is as relevant to the educational needs of the low achiever as any other pupil. In the words of Bruner:

> Good teaching that emphasizes the structure of a subject is probably even more valuable for the less able student than for the gifted one, for it is the former rather than the latter who is most easily thrown off the track by poor teaching.[13]

Bruner claims that the main difficulty for a child lies not so much in the structures of the subject disciplines as in the ways they are adapted and presented to the learner. In other words, the success of well intentioned aims will depend on the quality of the teaching, which must take into account the interests, learning difficulties and developmental stages of the children. More will be said about teaching strategies in later chapters.

What, then, are the distinctive features of historical knowledge which we should be endeavouring to teach children, including low achievers? Dr Rogers points out that historical knowledge, like all knowledge, has a three-fold character.[14] It is:

1 *Propositonal* – the product of historical enquiry, usually taking the form of an historical narrative. In a phrase, it is the 'know that' of history, which probably accounts for most of the learning done in schools
2 *Procedural* – the process of historical enquiry ('know how'), implying learning through doing. At the simplest level, procedures will demand reference skills such as the location of information from an index or library catalogue; at the highest level, they will demand all the skills of historical research, including the use of primary sources
3 *Conceptual* – the general notions and ideas that are basic to an understanding of both factual content and the methods of historical enquiry.

The three aspects of historical knowledge listed above are inter-related and inter-dependent. Indeed, key elements of historical knowledge may be seen to cut across such boundaries. The subject of historical imagination, which has attracted considerable specialist attention, is a case in point[15]. Defined succinctly as 'inference from evidence'[16], it is central to the whole historical process, is both cognitive and affective in nature, and defies neat classification into any single compartment of knowledge.

From our understanding of history as a subject discipline, it is possible to list a wide range of cognitive–intellectual aims for the teaching of history to children. The following list is eclectic in nature. Drawn from a number of sources[17], it is designed with low achievers in mind:

1 HISTORICAL SKILLS

1 *Factual knowledge* – the relatively simple acquisition and recall of facts.
2 *Comprehension* – understanding through:
   (a) translation – of information from one form to another;
   (b) interpretation – making out the meaning of information;
   (c) extrapolation – making forecasts about the development of a situation.
3 *Application* – of knowledge to a new problem.
4 *Analysis* – the skills of breaking information down into manageable parts and comparing and contrasting more than one piece of evidence.
5 *Synthesis* – the ability to build a piece of work from the selection of various sources and presenting it in original form.
6 *Judgement* – the assessment of reliability and bias in the evidence.
7 *Imagination* – inferences from evidence in terms of creating mental images, empathy and creativity in problem-solving.

2 BASIC ANCILLARY SKILLS

1 *Presentation* – especially the layout and structure of written work.
2 *Reading* – of textbooks and worksheets, etc.
3 *Writing* – style, spelling and basic grammar.
4 *Oral communication* – questioning, answering and discussing; the ability to listen; the use of mechanical aids such as tape-recorders.
5 *Developing memory and recall* – through revision techniques and study skills.
6 *Basic numeracy* – for coping with chronology, graphs and simple calculations.
7 *Mapping skills* – the points of the compass; scale; symbols, etc.

3 HISTORICAL CONCEPTS

1 *Source* – primary and secondary.
2 *Evidence* – with related concepts such as reliability, bias and truth.
3 *Historical time* – dates (BC and AD); centuries; ages and periods, etc.
4 *Cause and Consequence* – logical sequences in events.
5 *Continuity and Change* – through time.
6 *Vocabulary* – the correct understanding of words and expressions used in historical context.

There are also several cognitive–intellectual aims relating more specifically to subject content. These will be discussed in a later section on the syllabus (p. 44).

ESTABLISHING AIMS: THE AFFECTIVE–EMOTIONAL

The cognitive (thinking) and affective (feeling) domains are, in reality, inseparable. Indeed, it would be impossible to study history in a meaningful way 'unless the intellect were assisted and enriched by the affective powers.'[18] As Mary Warnock so rightly claims, the impetus behind any imaginative activity (so important to the study of history) comes as much from the emotions as from reason[19]. In the words of Coltham and Fines:

> Without the emotional involvement. . .the study of a subject – any subject – cannot really be said to have begun; and without such involvement, the study cannot fruitfully continue.[20]

For less able children, whose feelings may be damaged through a sense of failure or social disadvantage, emotional considerations take on a special significance. Our affective–emotional aims in teaching history should go some way to remedying these problems; but before discussing these, the problems themselves need to be more clearly specified.

First, there is a social problem which is more widespread than what we generally understand by the term 'social disadvantage'. It is aptly described by Hargreaves in his stimulating book as 'the decline of community'[21]. Its manifestations are many and varied: the demise of the extended family; the disappearance of the 'street' as a focal point of working-class community life; area development and re-housing in high-rise flats and council estates; a high incidence of divorce and single-parent families; families where both parents go out to work; material deprivation and mass youth unemployment; and a disturbing upward trend in the crime rate, especially among young offenders. The social message is clear: 'The youth subcultures, despite variations in form, all represented a kind of magical attempt to recover community.'[22] In arguing the case for teaching local history in schools, Dr W. B. Stephens states:

> A large number of children in an era of mobility of labour, of the destruction of old communities and the erection of new towns, new estates and new schools, find themselves intellectually and emotionally bereft of roots. . .Many thirst for the security of belonging to a comprehensible group of which they can be proud. They are, then, potentially interested in their own town and their own county.[23]

Anne and James Bromwich, speaking from direct experience of teaching children with severe social and emotional problems (like so many low achievers), are convinced that the children at CAVE Truancy Project gained immense value from the study of history:

> Learning history, to someone with little experience of the secure or long-term, offers a real sense that things can last; that people have lived many different ways, but that there are common features which hold us all together. A sense of time,

especially the great span of man's history, provides not only meaning to the past, but promise for the future: the continuity of humanity through time reinforces the sense of meaning for the present. In this sense history is a vital therapy: it helps put the children in touch with their own feelings and encourages an ability to see how people relate to each other. This can strike at the core of deep-seated phobias and insecurites, whether it be doubts of their own worth or some bitterly felt racial prejudice. Yet history teaches without threatening, as problems about man's behaviour are treated at one remove.[24]

One important aim, then, in the teaching of history should be to provide children with a stronger sense of social identity, enriched by an awareness of the past and an appreciation of heritage, and reinforced by visions of hope for the future.

A second problem arises from what Philip Jackson described as the 'hidden curriculum' – those values and attitudes passed on to children unintentionally by their teachers and the school system.[25] The problem is what Hargreaves calls an unwitting destruction of pupil dignity – dignity defined as 'a sense of being worthy, of possessing creative, inventive and critical capacities, of having the power to achieve personal and social change.'[26] Professor Skemp has argued that children are expected to succeed in a wide range of subjects which lie outside their immediate interests or spheres of competence. In all but a few subjects with which they feel a special affinity, pupils are engaged in an enduring battle against the disgrace of failure. In the words of Skemp:

> The pupil. . .is like a learner-swimmer who has been forcibly taken into the water by someone who himself likes swimming and is good at it, and considers it to be for the pupil's own good that he too should learn to swim. The pupil wants to be on dry land, in some situation of his own choice, not another's.[27]

This point can be applied with great force of conviction to the plight of the less able whose low level of attainment is likely to reinforce their sense of general inadequacy, frustration and anxiety. This is not simply a result of the children's weaknesses but a reflection of a narrowly cognitive–intellectual (especially literary) emphasis in our educational system and an equally narrow conception of human intelligence. Thus comments Hargreaves:

> The less able understand that they lack the very quality on which the school sets most score; a sense of failure tends to permeate the whole personality leaving a residue of powerlessness and hopelessness. It is here that dignity, as I have defined it, is most seriously damaged.[28]

It follows therefore that an important aim in our history teaching should be the promotion of a pupil's dignity or self-esteem. This will not be achieved by abolishing all those aspects of the curriculum with which the low achiever has difficulty; but we do need to build on children's strengths as much as we try to remedy their weaknesses. This can only be done by broadening the range of knowledge and skills that we value. As A. V. Kelly so rightly comments:

> We must show all pupils that educational enterprises do not always involve the skills of reading and writing, that other kinds of activity can be just as valuable, in some contexts more valuable, and that we do value these things.[29]

The implications for the history curriculum are enormous. The diversification of skills – already evident in the so-called 'New History' – will require a greater emphasis and refinement of the concrete and practical representations of the subject, so that low achievers will not only more readily comprehend but also find the study of history a more enjoyable and rewarding experience. These vital issues, which relate more specifically to the practice of teaching, will be discussed in later chapters.

By way of synthesis, the principal aims (affective–emotional) in teaching history to low achievers may be listed as follows:

1 *Enjoyment in learning* – this will deepen interest and a sense of commitment to study and therefore promote desirable conative (willing) behaviours, such as 'attending' and 'responding'. How far we succeed in achieving this will depend largely on relating human feeling and activity, as portrayed through history, to the feelings and emotions of the children. As Marjorie Reeves explains, these will vary with the ages of the children. The younger child (primary and lower secondary) is likely to be fascinated by tales of discovery and exploration, by role play and detective work. Older children, on the other hand, are likely to be more attracted by the emotions of love and hate, heroism and idealism[30]
2 *Personal awareness* – it is a truism to say that through learning more about other people we come to understand ourselves more fully. History provides the richest storehouse of human experience and an unrivalled opportunity to reflect on other people's feelings and actions
3 *Social awareness* – we have argued at length that history can provide a sense of social cohesion; of belonging to a community with a distinctive heritage and cultural identity
4 *Promotion of self-esteem* – it is paramount that the learning of history provides all children with a sense of worth and achievement. We are educating children to promote the joy of success, not the shame of failure
5 *Social interaction* – although individual work is important, children derive immense pleasure from the co-operative effort of working in groups; and it is through social interaction that we develop social competence. History should provide ample opportunity for this type of activity.

ESTABLISHING AIMS: THE SYLLABUS CONTENT

In a recent book, Geoffrey Partington has specified 'criteria of significance' which may be regarded as 'the most suitable principles to guide our choice of syllabus content'. Thus Partington would put the choice of any historical topic to the test on the basis of the following criteria:

1 Importance – to the people in the past
2 Profundity – how deeply people's lives have been affected
3 Quantity – how many lives have been affected

4 Durability – for how long people's lives have been affected
5 Relevance – in terms of the increased understanding of present life.[31]

This framework, although not without merit, poses two major problems. First, it is highly cognitive–intellectual in emphasis with no reference to the affective–emotional needs of children. Consequently, the history of hairdressing (in contrast to the history of industrialisation) would gain only a superficial rating according to Partington's second criterion[32]. However, contrast the following observation by Marjorie Reeves:

> Sometimes, indeed, the gap between present experience and what seems a proper syllabus is too great. A class of girls, school-leavers mostly, were ostensibly 'doing' Walpole, and the 'sleeping dogs' were indeed just lying: manifestly they were miles away. When asked what they wanted to do after leaving school they nearly all answered: 'Hairdressing'. A project on hairdressing through the ages sparked them off in a way that the evolution of Cabinet Government never would have, and at least they departed with their own picture of successive civilisations expressed in their styles of hair and clothes.[33]

I suppose one glib answer to this kind of dilemma would be to say that our history syllabus should consist only of those topics which are both profoundly interesting and profoundly important; but as any teacher knows this is easier said than done. If I had to take sides in this debate my support would go to Marjorie Reeves, for it is those children imbued with enthusiasm for the subject who are most likely to derive benefit from their studies. The second problem with Partington's criteria of significance is that they are too all-embracing to offer the teacher any real help in making a choice of syllabus content. The amount of recorded history that would satisfy the five criteria is prodigious, so we must look elsewhere for guidance on how to establish priorities and narrow the range of selection to manageable proportions.

A number of valuable guidelines and sample history syllabuses for the less able have already been published[34], but we must avoid being over-prescriptive. There are valid reasons why a common core history curriculum has never been recommended. To begin with, there is no *sine qua non* in the study of history. Each and every period and aspect of history can be defended on the school curriculum. Distant periods, for example, provide children with the stimulus of contrast, whereas contemporary history is arguably more immediate and utilitarian because of its close link with current affairs. It is also frequently stressed that the choice of content must reflect the interests of the teacher so that an infectious enthusiasm is more likely to be transmitted to the pupils. And finally, it goes without saying that all periods and aspects of history can be taught in such a way as to promote the essential skills and concepts discussed earlier in this chapter.

Notwithstanding these arguments, there is a growing concern for content for a number of reasons:

1 The skills and organising concepts (at a rudimentary classroom level) are not necessarily unique to a study of history. Evidence, empathy, analysis,

synthesis and the detection of bias can all be demonstrated in political studies, economics, human geography, literature and social studies. What is arguably unique is an historical perspective, especially an appreciation of continuity and change over time; but historical perspectives can be, and frequently are, incorporated into other subjects. History will be hard-pressed to justify its place on the curriculum as a separate subject on the grounds of skills and organising concepts alone

2 A judicious selection of content can more effectively achieve stated general aims. For example, family and local history is concrete and immediate for low achievers, and facilitates the use of field-work and the source method. Constitutional history, on the other hand, is highly abstract and generally regarded as unsuitable for such pupils

3 Some important aims have been expressed exclusively in terms of content; that is in terms of factual knowledge we think children ought to know. The *Schools Council History 13–16 Project*, for example, lists among its five 'needs' the need for adolescents to understand the world in which they live. The content implications of this aim are obvious from the inclusion of two studies from modern world history in the Project's CSE/GCE examination course

4 A more systematic approach to the choice of content can avoid wasteful repetition and overlap. In the words of Dr Hallam, 'the poor consumers can pass from the skin-clad cavemen to industrious Victorians twice in their school careers, once at primary and subsequently at secondary level.'[35] Although topics can be repeated in history at a greater level of sophistication, such repetition is hard to justify when many history syllabuses fall short of the twentieth century and fail to provide chidren with insights into contemporary issues

5 A careful selection of content can provide a balanced perspective of history. In the words of Dr John Fines: 'If, for example, I can ensure that. . .I can give my children a taste of history of all ages and places, and of history of all types. . .then I have at least tried to be fair to my subject and to the children.'[36]

What positive recommendations can be made in compiling a history syllabus for low achievers? First, following the arguments of Fines, a wide and balanced perspective of the subject should be offered. Not only will this provide variety and broaden the child's general knowledge, but also deepen the child's understanding of historical concepts. The nature of evidence, for example, varies with the period of history: archaeological finds are of vital importance to our understanding of ancient and medieval history, whereas the study of twentieth century history will require familiarity with vastly different sources of evidence, including archive film and newspapers. Secondly, certain aspects of history perphaps deserve greater emphasis. Two immediately spring to mind: the study of local history and the study of modern world history (particularly post-1945). Most pupils are curious about the history of their own locality because it is immediate. Local studies also provide ample opportunity for those concrete representations which make the subject more comprehensible and exciting for the pupils, whether these be history trails, local 'digs', museum visits or interviews with local residents – particularly elderly people. Local history is not easy to establish. It requires research and a gradual build up of resources and local contacts, but there are several published guides now available[37], and local libraries, museums, record offices and teachers' centres frequently offer invaluable assistance. The case for more recent world history is its relevance, in helping children to understand more of the contemporary world. There are certainly difficulties: many of the issues are highly complex and abstract, and many are so fresh that they have not yet received sufficient attention from the professional historians themselves. However, much can be gained from sample studies of conflict and co-operation; colourful biographies of great men and women; and discussions of current news items (e.g. wars, the rights of women and racial minorities, elections, unemployment, etc.) which can be placed in their historical context. Most less able children will have views on these issues – in all probability one-sided – so the history teacher will have achieved a lot if he/she has made them more respectful of evidence, a little more knowledgeable of the facts, and more tolerant in their outlook. Finally, careful attention must be paid to the structure of the content. Teachers may represent each of the following in their sampling: lines of development (e. g. medicine through the ages), which provide awareness of continuity and change; detective exercises (e.g. the mystery of Richard III and the missing princes), developing awareness of evidence and the historian's craft; biographies, a more concrete and human medium through which to understand something of the flavour of an age (e. g. the Revival of Learning through the life of Leonardo); outlines, perhaps a special period, through which to learn something of the causes and con-sequences of events; and studies in more depth, in order to promote empathy and imaginative insights.

Whatever the advice given or accepted, selection must always be rigorous, and the final decisions must rest with the departmental team. It is they who know best their own strengths and weaknesses, the interests and capabilities of their pupils, the potential of their local environment, and the extent of their budget and resources.

OBJECTIVES AND RATIONAL CURRICULUM PLANNING

Rational curriculum planning through objectives owes much to the influence of B. S. Bloom and his associates, whose taxonomy of educational aims and objectives is both behavioural and hierarchical. Thus the goals are arranged in sequence, so that the behaviours (skills acquired) at an elementary level will facilitate the mastery of more difficult skills at a higher level[38]. R. M. Gagné's approach is similar. His eight 'varieties' of learning, although more specifically related to learning conditions, are also arranged in a hierarchy: from 'signal learning', at the simplest level, to 'problem solving', at the most sophisticated[39]. Some years later, Coltham and Fines produced their famous pamphlet, which attempted to apply the objectives approach – in modified form – to the learning of history. The authors were clearly influenced by Bloom, and defined 'objective' in purely behavioural terms:

> An 'educational objective', then, describes firstly, what a learner can do as a result of having learned; and secondly it describes what an observer. . .can see the learner doing so that he can judge whether or not the objective has been successfully reached. And, thirdly, the objective, in describing what the learner will have achieved, also indicates what educational experience he requires if he is to achieve the objective.[40]

The objectives approach dominated much of the thinking behind the New History, with some undoubted benefits. Teachers were encouraged to think in terms of developing a much wider range of skills in their pupils; and the notion of a highly structured sequential learning programme had an obvious appeal to teachers of low achievers, for it now seemed possible to break down complex learning operations into relatively smooth, simple stages by utilising the principle of hierarchical organisation.

However, in recent years the objectives approach has come under increasing attack, both in general terms and, since the publication of the article by Gard and Lee[41], with specific reference to the teaching of history. Indeed, in a recent article, Dr Fines accepted many of the criticisms, although not to the point of disregarding his earlier work[42]. What, then, are the difficulties? First, it has been argued that the taxonomies are highly prescriptive and could relegate the teacher to the less creative role of curriculum implementer, rather than curriculum planner; in other words, little more than a docile agent in the educational process. Secondly, the approach is reductionist and may lead to a style of teaching which is mechanistic and laboriously dull. Thirdly, it has been stressed that the behavioural nature of the objectives is irrelevant to many educational processes, particularly those characterised by divergent, creative or open-ended thinking. Thinking is not observable, and there are many educational goals which cannot be accurately termed 'behavioural' because they cannot be observed, measured or precisely evaluated[43]. Many aspects of historical education fall into this category. Moreover, the unidimensional view of objectives as a guide to sequential learning is too simplistic, because each objective (e. g. comprehension) can be achieved at different levels of complexity and understanding. Finally, behavioural objectives, as defined by Coltham and Fines, are too learner-centred. Equal emphasis must be given to the conditions of learning, particularly teaching skills.

In spite of these criticisms, the objectives approach can be put to good use. First, the Coltham and Fines taxonomy or framework provides both a helpful 'checklist' and a 'map' of the whole field of the process of learning history in clear and precise terms. Thus, without being necessarily prescriptive, it is a useful reference work, reminding teachers of a wide range of skills and concepts that at some stage they should consciously develop in their pupils if their approach is to be a balanced one. Secondly, it must be said that much of the hostility to 'objectives' is semantic in nature – a rejection of the narrow focus on observable behaviour. It is perhaps more useful to view objectives in a wider context of learning conditions – as 'carefully structured programmes' or 'priority teaching and pupil learning intentions'. Hence in those circumstances where educational goals are virtually impossible to express in behavioural terms, objectives may be regarded as synonymous with 'the description of essential experiences and situations to which pupils should be exposed' in order to create optimal learning conditions[44]. No one could really disagree with a structured approach to teaching which emphasised carefully planned intervention on the part of the teacher to assist the child with learning problems; and objectives thus re-defined would, I believe, remove the sting from much of the opposition.

The claim that an objectives approach aids sequential learning needs examining in more detail. The principles of this so-called 'mastery learning' may be summarised as follows:

1 The subject is broken down into small working units, with unit objectives clearly defined
2 The first unit or graded step should be below the pupil's existing level of competence. Only then can the teacher ascertain when the child *first* encounters difficulty. Moreover, the initial task will relate to what the child already knows and can accomplish, so progress is smooth and painless, and motivation and reinforcement will result from the initial success
3 Formative or diagnostic tests are administered at the end of each unit to see if the unit has been mastered before proceeding to the next
4 In the event of a child failing to master a particular task, 'correctives' are used, including some or all of the following: small group sessions; in-dividualised tutoring (if necessary with another teacher to add new instructional perspectives – with obvious implications for team-teaching and co-operation between the Remedial and other departments); re-teaching (going over the points again); and the use of alternative learning materials.[45]

Clearly this approach is most appropriate for teaching those subjects which can be broken down into well-defined sequential units, requiring thinking of a more convergent kind. Consequently, it has been most strongly advocated for the teaching of the basic ancillary skills allied to history – in particular the fundamental skills of language. It has been reported, for example, how programmed learning assists pupils in quickly mastering the necessary vocabulary for history lessons[46]; and computer-assisted learning in reading and language development is already under way. The development of computer programmes more specifically related to the learning of history is an exciting prospect for further research.[47]

Nevertheless, the application of behavioural objectives (through such techniques as 'mastery learning') to the development of historical skills and concepts *per se* must be treated with great caution. The use of Bloom's hierarchy, for example, runs the risk of resurrecting the old fashioned notion that facts (knowledge) are for younger children and the less able, whereas the higher skills and concepts (e.g. judgement and an awareness of primary evidence) are for the gifted and more experienced student. Following Bruner's line of reasoning, there is no reason why this should be so. At each level, within the bounds of the type of thinking appropriate to the child's stage of development, every aspect of history can be utilised. Thus, for example, a child may well develop the concept of evidence and powers of judgement through handling material of a visual or concrete nature, but find great difficulty in coping with lower level skills and concepts if presented in an abstract way. Sequential learning, then, must take into account what Bruner calls the three 'modes of representation': the enactive (learning through the sensory activities of 'doing'), the iconic (learning through visual imagery) and the symbolic (learning in a more abstract way through the conventional symbols of language). These modes are not meant to be strictly age-bound, but interact at every stage of a child's education. However, a child's stage of cognitive development and readiness for learning will determine which mode should be emphasised. It is the teacher's task to represent the subject structure in terms of how the child views things. [48]

CONCLUSION

History teachers can no longer afford to be content with a merely intuitive belief in the value of their subject for all pupils. Evidence suggests that the teaching of history to low achievers in many schools leaves much to be desired. Moreover, the question of accountability and the growing concern with the need to link school more closely to the world of work and the responsibilities of adulthood means that a wide range of ostensibly more practical subjects could rival history for a place on an already heavily loaded curriculum. It is for these reasons that the teaching of history to low achievers must be justified through carefully planned aims and objectives which provide a sense of purpose and clarity of direction.

In responding to this challenge, history teachers should be encouraged by the recent statement by Sir Keith Joseph, the Secretary of State for Education, at a conference of the Historical Association in February, 1984. Sir Keith argued that history has an essential and unique role in the common core curriculum for all pupils:

> . . .I am quite clear that we must arrive at a broadly agreed view of what should be offered to all pupils, and what should additionally be available to some. I am clear that history is an essential component of the curriculum of *all* pupils. . . Of course history will appear in different forms in the curriculum according to the ages of pupils, just as those offering it should differentiate between their abilities. . . . But it should be present throughout the primary and secondary phases up to age 16:

and this should be made explicit in any future statements of curricular objectives for the primary as well as for the secondary phase.[49]

According to Sir Keith, major aims of history teaching should include an understanding of society (through a study of families, communities and nations) and a greater emphasis on the use of evidence and its interpretation:

> In short, history properly taught, justifies its place in the school curriculum by what it does to prepare all pupils for the responsibilities of citizenship as well as the demands of employment and the opportunities of leisure[50]

Many of these aims and objectives are demonstrated in Ben Kerwood's proposed history syllabus for a core curriculum in the new Certificate of Pre-Vocational Education (CPVE) at 17-plus. Kerwood's proposals are geared towards satisfying the requirements of less academic students, based on 'vocational needs, transferable skills, experiential learning and negotiated curricula which imply some shift in the control of learning from teacher to learner'.[51] In line with the Further Education Curriculum Development Unit's common core objectives in *A Basis for Choice* (1979), Kerwood both outlines a suitable course and provides a more detailed discussion of a key unit – the family history project – by way of example. The aims of the project are to help adolescents to understand their own place in, and contribution towards, their family and local community; to lead them to ask wider questions about their society and to cultivate an interest in the problems of the contemporary world; and to apply the skills of historical investigation (e.g. the observation, identification and evaluation of evidence) in a way which is primary and tangible. Thus much of the work would be envisaged taking place outside the school or college in the form of interviews, surveys and visits to places of historical interest. Kerwood's proposals are convincing and highly relevant to the whole question of teaching history to lower ability or less academic children. Above all, it shows – in my opinion beyond any reasonable doubt – that history has a relevance to all youngsters and can be taught in such a way that it is highly practical and easily accessible. In satisfying the needs for a broad social and political education, Kerwood's proposals exemplify many of the aims and objectives of community studies discussed earlier this chapter in the context of David Hargreaves' work.

Many of the aims discussed in the course of this chapter apply to the teaching of history to all children; and Evelyn Cowie rightly makes the assertion that 'our primary object is surely the same for all pupils to give them an understanding of the society in which they live, and therefore an appreciation of its historical context'.[52] However, special educational needs, in regard to both age and ability, must be met through the execution of specific objectives. Although behavioural objectives have a part to play, particularly in the mastery of basic skills, their limitations have been noted. How far well-intentioned aims and objectives can be achieved depends on how successfully they relate to the actual practice of teaching; and this will be the focus of attention in subsequent chapters.

REFERENCES

1 G. R. Elton, *The practice of history*. Fontana, 1967, p. 182
2 For example, G. H. Bantock, *Dilemmas of the curriculum*. Martin Robertson, 1980, chap. 5
3 M. Warnock, *Schools of thought*. Faber, 1977, p. 82
4 P. H. Hirst, 'The logic of the curriculum'. *Journal of Curriculum Studies*, 2 1969, p. 153
5 M. Skilbeck, 'Core curriculum – a fresh approach'. *Primary Education Review*, 12, 1981
6 See, for example, M. Golby et al (eds.), *Curriculum design*. Croom Helm, 1975; DES *Curriculum 11–16*. HMSO, 1977
7 D. H. Hargreaves, *The challenge for the comprehensive school*. Routledge & Kegan Paul, 1982, p. 133
8 P. H. Hirst, *op. cit.*, p. 154
9 W. Brennan, *Curricular needs of slow learners*. Evans/Methuen, 1979, p. 41
10 W. Brennan, *Shaping the education of slow learners*. Routledge & Kegan Paul 1974, p. 86
11 P. H. Hirst, *op. cit*
12 P. J. Rogers and F. Aston, 'Play, enactive representation and learning'. *Teaching History*, 19, 1977, p. 18
13 J. Bruner, *The process of education*. Harvard, 1960, p. 9
14 P. J. Rogers, *The new history: theory into practice*. Historical Association 1979, chap. 1
15 See, for example, A. J. Boddington, 'Empathy and the teaching of history'. *British Journal of Educational Studies*, vol. 28, no.1, 1980; H. J. Eadson, The use of the imagination in the learning and teaching of history, unpublished MEd dissertation, University of Exeter, 1979; V. Little, 'What is historical imagination?' *Teaching History*, 36, 1983
16 A. Gard and P. J. Lee, '"Educational objectives for the study of history" Reconsidered'. In A. K. Dickinson and P. J. Lee (eds.), *History teaching and historical understanding*. Heinemann, 1978, p. 33
17 See, for example, J. Coltham and J. Fines, *Educational objectives for the study of history*. Historical Association, 1971; D. Gunning, *The teaching of history*. Croom Helm, 1978; V. McIver (ed.), *Teaching history to slow-learning children in secondary schools*. Belfast, 1982; M. Palmer, 'Educational objectives and source materials: some practical suggestions'. *Teaching History*, 16, 1976
18 B. Garvey and M. Krug, *Models of history teaching in the secondary school*. Oxford, 1977, p. 14
19 Quoted by V. Little, *op. cit.*, p. 32
20 J. Coltham and J. Fines, *op. cit.*, p. 5
21 D. H. Hargreaves, *op. cit.*, chap. 2
22 *Ibid.*, p. 37
23 W. B. Stephens, *Teaching local history*. Manchester University Press, 1977, pp. 13–14
24 A. Bromwich and J. Bromwich, 'Teaching history to truants'. *What Next?*, vol. 1, no.4 1982
25 P. Jackson, *Life in classrooms*. Holt, Rinehart & Winston, 1968
26 D. H. Hargreaves, *op. cit.*, p. 17
27 R. R. Skemp, *Intelligence, learning and action*. John Wiley, 1979, p. 275
28 D. H. Hargreaves, *op. cit.*, pp. 62–63
29 A. V. Kelly, *Mixed-ability grouping: theory and practice*. Harper & Row, 1978, p. 105
30 M. Reeves, *Why history?*. Longman, 1980, p. 50

31 G. Partington, *The idea of an historical education.* NFER, 1980, pp. 112–116, 136

32 *Ibid.*, p. 113

33 M. Reeves, *op. cit.*, p. 50

34 See, for example, K. Hodgkinson, *Designing a history syllabus for slow-learning children.* Historical Association (n.d.); V. McIver (ed.), *op. cit.*, pp. 186–206

35 R. Hallam, 'History'. In M. Hinson and M. Hughes (eds.), *Planning effective progress.* Hulton, 1982

36 J. Fines, 'Towards some criteria for establishing the history curriculum 8–13'. *Teaching History*, 31, 1981

37 An extensive bibliography is provided by W. B. Stephens, *op. cit*

38 B. S. Bloom et al, *Taxonomy of educational objectives handbook one: cognitive domain.* New York, 1956

39 R. M. Gagné, *The conditions of learning.* Holt, Rinehart & Winston, 1965

40 J. Coltham and J. Fines, *op. cit.*, pp. 3–4

41 A. Gard and P. J. Lee, *op. cit*

42 J. Fines, 'Educationl objectives for history – ten years on' *Teaching History*, 30, 1981

43 See, for example, D. Hogben, 'The behavioural objectives approach: some problems and dangers'. *Journal of Curriculum Studies*, 4, 1972; D. Lawton, *Social change, educational theory and curriculum planning.* London, 1973; L. Stenhouse, *An introduction to curriculum research and development.* Heinemann, 1975

44 W. Brennan, *op. cit.*, 1979, p. 162

45 J. H. Block (ed.), *Mastery learning: theory and practice.* Holt, Rinehart & Winston, 1970

46 J. Coltham, *The development of thinking and the learning of history.* Historical Association, 1971, pp. 38–39

47 A more detailed discussion is provided in Chapter 5

48 J. Bruner, *op. cit.*, p. 33

49 K. Joseph, 'Why teach history in school?'. *The Historian*, no. 2, 1984, p. 10

50 *Ibid.*, p. 12

51 B. Kerwood, 'The certificate of pre-vocational education – what the history teacher can contribute'. *Teaching History*, 38, 1984, p. 3

52 E. Cowie, *History and the slow-learning child.* 1979, p. 9

4

Language and Communication

INTRODUCTION

Of all the learning difficulties that low achievers encounter, the failure to master the use of language – and therefore the inability to communicate effectively – must be one of the most serious. This is particularly true in the case of history, as Professor Burston points out:

> In history teaching we are dependent to quite an exceptional degree on ordinary language as our medium of communication. History, more than any other school subject, depends upon literacy in its pupils as a prerequisite to success, and increased literacy is perhaps its most important by-product.[1]

Dr Coltham has described language as 'the enabling factor in learning' – the means whereby children attain higher level concepts[2]; and D. G. Watts, following Vygotsky, makes the bold assertion that:

> Thought is not merely expressed in words; it comes into existence through them. . . . This proposition in itself would direct our attention away from a preoccupation with concrete objects and activity, and towards pedagogic methods and subjects which employ language.[3]

Although Watts is surely right to emphasise the importance of language, teachers should not discredit the use of 'concrete objects and activity' in the education of pupils with learning difficulties. Indeed, they are not inseparable from the development of linguistic skills: there must be a delicate fusion of language with other agents of the learning process in order to create balance and the optimal conditions for effective learning.

The quotations above foreshadowed the recent interest in developing language across the curriculum, especially since the publication of the Bullock Report in 1975, which stressed that all subject teachers need to be aware of:

1 The linguistic processes by which their pupils acquire information and understanding, and the implications for the teachers' own use of language.
2 The reading demands of their own subjects, and ways in which the pupils can be helped to meet them.[4]

In spite of the enthusiasm with which many schools have taken up the challenge[5], evidence would suggest that they have not been very successful in meeting the needs of pupils with learning difficulties (see Chapter 2).

The purpose of this chapter is to examine in some detail the problems of language and communication, and to suggest various strategies of remediation and new approaches to the teaching of the subject.

LANGUAGE PRESENTATION AND PUPIL COMPREHENSION

In terms of the way language is presented, low achievers are faced with three inter-related problems: the linguistic demands of history as a subject discipline; the high level of readability of course materials; and the teacher's use of language in general exposition. Each of these difficulties can be examined in more detail.

The various school subjects place different linguistic demands on children: 'Each discipline has its own body of concepts and vocabulary, its own style of writing, and its own style of organizing and presenting information.'[6] The set of linguistic features associated with a particular discipline are commonly referred to as the *subject register*. Bernbaum (1972), Edwards (1978) and Levine (1981) have made pioneering studies of language and the teaching of history, drawing attention to a number of problems. First, history presents a proliferation of abstract terms and concepts, such as 'revolution', 'democracy', 'social distress' and 'Sick Man of Europe'; secondly, its lack of a specialised vocabulary and reliance on everyday language 'leaves pupils unusually dependent on the language they bring with them.'[7] Consequently, ambiguity and confusion can arise over meanings associated with the simplest words and phrases, such as the case of the girl who thought that Wolsey had shot the Pope because he aimed at the papacy[8]. Confusion is even more likely when the precise referents of words alter in their historical context. Historical documents, for example, which contain words such as 'factory' cannot be properly understood if we ascribe twentieth-century meanings to such words. This raises the whole question of the suitability of primary sources, particularly manuscripts, for children of low attainment. Difficult texts, primary or otherwise, will almost certainly compound the sense of frustration for low achievers; and teachers who envisage using such sources will be well advised to modify the text: to transform historical *sources* into educational *resources*[9]. Harry Allen recommends the presentation of historical documents at three levels of difficulty:

1 A photostat copy of the original document
2 A verbatim typescript
3 A simplified version in typescript

All three versions can be presented to the class for discussion and comparison, so that even the least able pupils are not denied the instinctive curiosity and interest that is so often triggered off by access to primary sources. However, as Harry Allen so rightly points out:

> Assuming that the teacher is concerned to avoid the pupil being frustrated by the difficulty of the language, the biggest danger is losing faith with the original. If the personality of the document is changed much of the point of using it is lost.[10]

From recent evidence on the high levels of readability of history textbooks and other course materials, it has been argued that the demands on many children – and slow-learning children in particular – are unrealistic[11]. This evidence is based on the application of numerous readability tests, which are mainly American in origin, and rely principally on the criteria of sentence length and the number of syllables in words. The calculations are then converted to grade levels and/or reading ages by way of the various formulae, such as the Smog formula, Gunning's Fog Index, Flesch's Reading Ease formula and the Dale-Chall formula[12]. The cloze procedure, which can be used as an alternative, operates on a different principle: words are omitted from a sample of the text, and the children asked to fill in the gaps with suitable words to indicate their level of understanding. The cloze procedure therefore tests, rather than predicts, reading difficulties. Although readability tests may serve as a useful guide for teachers in selecting suitable material, especially for poor readers, they have severe limitations and should be used with caution. Basically these limitations result from the omission of important variables, which are either too difficult or too time-consuming to assess objectively. The general limitations may be listed as follows:

1 Grammatical complexity is not adequately measured by the readability tests; long sentences and multi-syllabic words are not always the most difficult to read or to comprehend. Although Dale drew up an extensive list of familiar words, this can no longer be regarded as appropriate for British children in the 1980's[13]. Anaphoric references (including words such as 'he' and 'she', and phrases such as 'the above' and 'defined earlier') can cause confusion if used inappropriately, although this would not be evident from the readability formulae.

2 Readability tests also fail to reveal the difficulties resulting from the terseness of style in most historical writing. In contrast to the story or novel, the history textbook or worksheet contains a heavy concentration of factual information and concepts. Consequently, W. Kintsch has advocated the use of propositional analysis as a better index of sentence difficulty[14]. Consider, for example, the two following sentences by way of contrast:

(a) Romulus, the legendary founder of Rome, took the women of the Sabine by force. (Four propositions)
(b) Cleopatra's downfall lay in her foolish trust of the fickle political figures of the Roman world. (Eight propositions)[15]

The main problem is that this type of analysis is very time-consuming, but it is one approach to quantifying information structure or 'idea density' – an elusive factor in readability research. Terseness of style can also result in the most stringent economy in the use of words of explanation and a mistaken assumption on the part of writers that their readers share in all kinds of previous knowledge. This can create a formidable barrier to comprehension – even of those passages which utilise the simplest syntax and choice of vocabulary. The point is very well illustrated by Nick Levine, who contrasts and analyses two extracts on the Tolpuddle Martyrs from a couple of history textbooks: one by Purton, the other by Newth[16]. It is the latter, despite its detail and use of some difficult words, which earns the more favourable review. In short:

> The author has maintained the momentum of the story, avoided words that are likely to be a barrier to comprehension, and included the detail necessary for a focussed understanding. She invites the readers to enjoy the story in language that she shares with them.[17]

I was even more convinced when I asked a group of 13 year olds (of low academic ability) for their opinions about the two extracts. They agreed unanimously with the choice of Nick Levine. As one girl put it: 'I like the second story because it gives you lots more detail and tells you more about the people.' This leads us to the third limitation of readability tests; that of human interest and motivation.

3 There is clear evidence that poor readers can surprise their teachers by reading with understanding and enthusiasm books which, in terms of vocabulary and syntax, would normally be regarded as too difficult. The reason for this is a high level of motivation.[18] In other words, to quote the old proverb, where there is a will there is a way; and children who find the subject content of value and interest are more certain to provide the will to succeed. In the words of Colin Harrison:

> If children can gain an insight into such concepts as justice and truth, for example, by consulting and discussing extracts from difficult books, including primary sources to which such less able students do not normally have access, then the materials will have served their purpose.[19]

It must also be emphasised that books which satisfy the requirements of the readability formulae run the risk of using language which is flat and monotonous. Boring, uninspiring sentences are difficult to avoid when rigid constraints are imposed on sentence length and the choice of words. There is thus a real danger that pupil curiosity and motivation may be sacrificed in the interests of immediate comprehension. All children, including low achievers, need to be stretched if they are to find their work a worthwhile challenge. However, this should never reach the point of frustration. Like so many difficult issues, striking the right balance is critically important; and this can only be achieved through detailed knowledge and experience of the children in question. The teacher's judgement of the situation is all-important.

4 Finally, it should be noted that the reliability of readability tests is open to question, particularly in measuring one test against another, and where samples are small[20].

Helping children to overcome their problems in reading history texts is far from easy, but the teacher can take the initiative in the selection of the most appropriate materials available, and in the design of worksheets and work-cards. The following suggestions should help towards finding a solution:

1 Applying readability tests, but at the same time bearing in mind their limitations
2 Finding out what the children think of a particular text. Colin Harrison suggests that the pupils are invited to underline sections on a photostat copy in a colour code; for example, easy sections in blue; difficult sections in red. The teacher can then assess the suitability of the material for that particular group of children, and perhaps collect together – throughout the course of the year – lists of words and phrases which have caused the most difficulty. These can then constitute a glossary in booklet form and made available to future classes of similar ability for reference[21]
3 Where possible, reducing the concentration of facts and concepts in any given passage of history. Instead, a few key concepts can provide the core of a story or a readable narrative, to which the child can relate more easily. In brief, a compromise has to be reached between the two extremes of reading material which Roe and his associates define as *content* and *narrative* readers
4 Drawing more attention to key words in the text. Such words, especially if they are unfamiliar, can be listed separately (perhaps at the head of the worksheet) for discussion and clarification. They may also be indicated in bold type as they occur in the text, and repeated more frequently as an aid to reinforcement
5 Where possible linking the text to visual stimuli to deepen understanding.

In conclusion, it must be remembered that readability formulae are only one tool of many in assessing the overall suitability of reading material. In the words of M. Hinson:

> Although readability formulas produce reasonably accurate estimates of reading difficulty, based on vocabulary and sentence structure, they do not measure the quality of style, conceptual levels, imagery in writing, nor can they predict the readers' interest. They are intended to complement teachers' trained judgement and experience, rather than supersede them.[22]

Finally, we can now examine the third major difficulty in language presentation: that of the teacher's use of language in general exposition. There are some widely accepted principles for any teacher of low achievers, including: the use of simple vocabulary; the avoidance of abstract terms; the use of short sentences and paragraphs with simple syntax; and the presentation of work-sheets with large print, double-spacing and sections broken with diagrams and illustrations.

An equally important principle is for the teacher to relate the learning task to the children's existing knowledge and experience. The dangers otherwise are spelled out by Dr Coltham: 'If the gap between the known and the new is too great, the individual can only either ignore the new – or perhaps more correctly, fail to notice it – or distort it. . . '[23] To facilitate such a transition, *advance organisers* can be used: 'Sets of ideas which are presented to the learner in advance of the body of meaningful material to be learned, in order to ensure that the relevantly anchoring ideas will be available.'[24] In other words, the organisers provide the learner with a cognitive anchor to which new knowledge can be attached. D. P. Ausubel distinguishes between two types of advance organiser: the *comparative* and the *expository*. The former are direct links between the learning task and what the child already knows; for example, the development of historical understanding through family or local history or through the use of analogies, all of which are already familiar to the child. Professor Edwin Peel provides a good example of an analogy between a boxing bout and the English Civil War[25]:

Analogy (familiar)	*Historical Scenario (unfamiliar)*
Boxing Bout	Civil War
Experienced, tired boxer	Charles I
Lack of stamina	Shortage of funds
Loss of speed	Drying up of resources
Experience	Trained army
Predictable outcomes	Predictable outcomes

History provides unlimited scope for the use of such analogies, and most history teachers have a substantial repertoire. On the other hand, expository organisers are intermediate links which have to be taught in their own right, and act as bridges between the child's limited experience and the demands of the learning task. Expository organisers are therefore both didactic and predominantly linguistic in nature, and usually take the form of definitions and explanations of new or unfamiliar words and concepts.

In view of what has already been said about the readability of many history textbooks, it is likely that they will present more serious obstacles to comprehension than carefully designed worksheets; and yet, because of pressures of time and resources, low achievers will be expected to use them. Indeed, it is important that they learn to do so, in order to develop reference skills, reading ability and a measure of independence in their study of history. Careful instruction on the part of the teacher can certainly help to mitigate some of the problems that low achievers encounter in using textbooks; for example, the teacher can:

1 Define clearly, and limit the scope of, the reading assignments, e.g. 'Read the second paragraph on page 10', or 'Read the first six lines on page 14'
2 List two or three main ideas from the reading assignment on the blackboard or overhead projector, thus helping the children to focus their attention on the most salient points
3 Define and discuss any difficult or unfamiliar words or concepts in the passage.

Having discussed the problems arising from the presentation of language to low achievers, we can now examine the difficulties associated with the way that children are expected to use written language.

CHILDREN'S USE OF WRITTEN LANGUAGE

It is important to stress the recommendations of the Writing Research Survey of the Schools Council: that children should have the opportunity to express themselves in a greater variety of styles of writing[26]. When writing is a concomitant of varied learning activities, this should follow as a matter of course. Simulations and games, for example, provide scope for introducing a greater element of expressive writing. The written work demanded of low achievers should include the following:

1 *Description* – of pictures, objects, historical sites and other primary material. This form of writing should act as a reinforcement to visual perception, with an emphasis on accuracy and keen observation. Pupils should be encouraged to make comparisons; for example, between photographs of street scenes in Victorian times and the present day
2 *Recording* – of notes either on field trips or in the classroom, for the purpose of providing a framework for future reference
3 *Expressive writing* – to accompany such activities as drama, games and simulations. Such writing could include the reports of group discussions (for the benefit of the whole class) and the summaries of debates
4 *Imaginative writing* – in the form of historical narrative, plays, diaries and newspaper reports, etc., based on rich stimuli.

It can be readily appreciated that these different styles of writing present different levels of difficulty for low achievers. Bearing in mind the limitations of rational curriculum planning (see Chapter 3), it is nevertheless possible to suggest a hierarchy of educational tasks that will hopefully promote sequential learning in language acquisition and the development of historical understanding. Exercises may take the pattern outlined below.

1 ESTABLISHING A KEY VOCABULARY

This can be taken to mean a pupil's ability to recognise and display an awareness of the most basic words, facts and concepts for an understanding of the historical passage in question. For the functionally illiterate, it may be necessary to develop a sight vocabulary of essential words and names through the use of pictures with matching words and flashcards: techniques which are well known to remedial specialists. The sight vocabulary can be reinforced in a number of ways, including the rearrangement of words with jumbled letters, the completion of crosswords, colouring word puzzles (see Fig. 4.1), and 'modified scrabble' exercises (see Fig. 4.2). A more advanced task is for the child to insert key words into gaps in sentences which will provide the necessary meaning or definition. Such an exercise tests the child's ability to reason at an elementary level through being able to place key words/names in the correct context. Care must be taken in the construction of such exercises; for example, the two following sentences present different levels of difficulty for the pupil:

Fig. 4.1 Colouring a Word Puzzle

I	N	F	A	N	T	R	Y	E
Q	M	O	N	F	R	H	P	G
S	T	V	Z	K	E	L	R	M
W	N	P	A	N	N	P	E	O
E	B	D	C	R	C	S	S	T
A	U	W	S	X	H	Y	J	I
P	Z	J	A	B	E	C	T	F
O	O	Q	G	A	S	H	A	D
N	R	H	N	M	I	J	N	E
S	O	M	M	E	L	K	K	G

Fig. 4.2 A Modified Scrabble Exercise

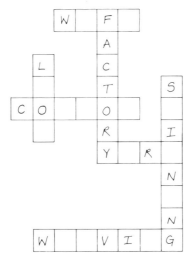

(a) William of Normandy won the battle of . . . .
(b) The Battle of . . . . was won by William of Normandy.

The second exercise is more difficult because backward readers frequently lack, or do not use, the skill of 'reading on' and 'retracing steps' in a passage to place a word in context or to analyse its meaning. The child will, in fact, have to read sentence (b) twice before being able to fill in the name 'Hastings', whereas the first sentence (a) need only be read once. For this reason, in the initial stages teachers should avoid a style of writing which puts the explanations of one sentence into later sentences or sections of the text. Before making this demand, the history teacher must develop the pupils' skills of reading ahead and re-reading the text. There is no reason why this should not be accomplished in a relatively short time (as long as the reading material is within the grasp of the pupils) but it is a fundamental skill that needs pointing out and which is too often overlooked. Other techniques that may be used to good effect include the matching of key words to given definitions presented in jumbled order – a 'heads and tails' exercise; the application of key words by making up sentences in which they are used correctly; and, at a more advanced stage, the researching of definitions from dictionaries and reference books. This will depend on the pupils' knowledge of a wide range of reference skills (e.g. the alphabet, indexes) and the ability to select the definition most appropriate to the history text being studied.

There is a real danger of overdoing vocabulary exercises, which are no more than a means to an end. The target objective is not the ability to master word puzzles but the development of historical understanding. The point can be nicely illustrated by a story told to me recently by the Head of History in a large comprehensive school in Norfolk. During a lesson to fourth-year low achievers on recent developments in Zimbabwe (an attempt to link history with current affairs and newspaper headlines) the name 'Mugabe' was written on the blackboard in bold capital letters. David, with an eager expression, raised his hand for the first time. The teacher, delighted at the apparent breakthrough in capturing the boy's attention, asked David to make his point, to which the reply (in all seriousness) was:

'Sir, have you not noticed that MUGABE spells E–BA–GUM backwards?'

David had certainly displayed an awareness of regional dialect and a certain panache for solving anagrams, but he had clearly missed the point of his history lesson.

2 SEQUENCING

Sequencing exercises entail the copying of sentences (presented in a random fashion) in the correct order. The result should be a logical, coherent historical narrative, without having tested the child's linguistic skills too severely. The narrative should provide the pupils with a model for clear writing, the style of which could be emulated when they progress to more independent writing. Such sequencing skills are particularly important as the 'organising principle' of history, encouraging pupils to read carefully, and serving as valuable diagnoses of pupils' logical reasoning. In a recent article, John Hull provides a good example, whereby pupils have to rearrange six sentences on an historical event, presenting them in correct sequence. Clues are provided in the phrasing of the sentences and in the inclusion of some key dates.[27]

3 FUNCTIONAL WRITING

The purpose of this type of writing is purely utilitarian. It may be formal, such as the recording of accurate information for future reference, or the submission of work for the purpose of assessment; it may also be informal, such as rough jottings for the purpose of exploring new ideas and structuring thoughts. It is to be expected that writing of the functional kind will never be too demanding in terms of length. Brevity and relevance are what should be sought by teacher and pupil alike. The work will then appear useful without being too onerous.

4 CREATIVE WRITING

Exercises on the lines of creative writing should be designed to cultivate the imagination and develop the more aesthetic aspects of linguistic expression, taking such form as the writing of simple plays and short stories in a narrative style. Above all, this kind of writing should be regarded as a pleasure: a means of assisting children to write what they want to write, and to want to write more. If, at some stage, low achievers are expected to write longer pieces of work, the creative mode is likely to be the most rewarding and effective means of achieving some measure of success. The children will, of course, require a number of props. Class or group discussions, and the listing of some basic historical details and ideas for a story will certainly help the child prior to an assignment in creative writing. This is very important, because, all too often, imaginative reconstruction is prone to flights of fancy. Primary sources, particularly detailed illustrations and extracts from diaries, eye-witness accounts and newspaper reports, can provide both the stimulus for a good story and a respect for evidence and realism. Providing the class with the opening sentence or paragraph of a story and asking them to complete it is also an effective technique. The pupils will also need help with the presentation and structuring of the work. R. Binns makes the useful suggestion that the left-hand page of the exercise book should be used for 'expressive' writing (rough notes and the listing of words, definitions and ideas) and the right-hand page for the drafting of sentences and paragraphs. The children will then be able to compare at a glance, without turning over the page, their own use of language in different forms, and see how words can be changed and rearranged to make more sense. Thus the children will take an active part in the correction and development of their own written language[28].

Of course, many of the writing skills discussed above must be developed in parallel; to a significant degree they must interact and overlap. However, in broad outline, the four stages (from vocabulary acquisition to creative writing) provide a framework for sequential learning with regard to the study of any given topic in history. Some of these points can be illustrated by the two sample worksheets (see Appendix C) which were first published in *Teaching History* [29]. The first worksheet is pitched very much at the level of 'describer' thinking. The first question attempts to place the exercise into some time scale, demanding simple calculations, whereas question 2 utilises the popular missing words technique. An important aim of the exercise is to train pupils to observe carefully; for example, by finding the names of the shopkeeper and the street and the number of people in the picture. However, question 5 and 6 provide some scope for imaginative and open-ended thinking. A worksheet such as this could be used in a variety of schemes. It could constitute part of a topic or centre of interest, part of a course on local history, or part of a unit on the meaning of history, illustrating the importance of primary and pictorial sources. Writing is encouraged through a response to a visual stimulus, important not only because it is concrete but also because it is a primary source of historical evidence.

The second worksheet has been designed with a number of features which should be of help to low achievers.

1 To some extent, it engineers the lesson format. The first section, 'Talking Point', provides a springboard for discussion that relates to the children's own experiences.

2 The worksheet is broken down into short sections and sub-headings. The diary entries facilitate this; and any which may prove too difficult for a particular group can be omitted with no serious overall loss. Each entry can be regarded as a unit for discussion in its own right.

3 The worksheet incorporates the principle of *advance organisers*. The first two paragraphs, relating the theme to the children's personal experiences, act as comparative organisers. Expository organisers are anticipated by including the more difficult or key words in capital letters. These should be the focus of preparatory discussion and clarification.

4 The style is not cramped by a concentration of difficult concepts or a proliferation of major historical events. With the exception of a few political commentaries, most of the entries are concerned with aspects of social life, with which the low achiever can more easily empathise.

5 The reading age of the worksheet (Gunning's Fog Index) is approximately 9.6 – well within the scope of most secondary children.

6 The questions are graded in difficulty, ranging from simple heads-and-tails exercises to tabulations and longer pieces of prose writing. These more demanding tasks are supported by many props and clues, especially questions 4, 7 and 8.

Sample worksheets and workcards are also to be found in several recent publications on low achievers[30].

Finally, a few words of caution need to be said about project work. This is perhaps the most advanced form of written work that could ever be expected of low achievers, for it combines most literary skills and demands synthesis. In the words of John Hull:

> Synthesis skills involve the ability to organise materials drawn from several sources to make a unified account. In exercising these skills in a form structured to suit children who find some difficulty in organising material, we are requiring a

higher form of comprehension as the pupil surveys and selects relevant material from differing and distracting sources . . . . For less able children this skill is hard at first.

There is certainly much to recommend project work: pupils can work at their own pace, they can pursue their own interests (an aid to motivation), and the teacher is able to circulate, offering individual guidance while the other children are fully occupied. However, project work is often disappointing through lack of adequate preparation. The success of project work with low achievers will depend on:

1 The teacher's realisation that it is a demanding and sophisticated exercise. It is unlikely to succeed until pupils have first mastered the more basic literary skills listed above
2 The adequate provision of materials to support either group or individual work (including reference books with an appropriate reading age)
3 Outlining a specific programme to follow (perhaps with accompanying worksheets) suggesting lines of enquiry and methods of presentation. Reference skills are extremely important in this respect
4 Plans for completion: how much is expected of each group and individual; and how the work is to be presented; for example, as a wall display, in booklet form, or as an exhibition for a parents' evening.

Projects should enable pupils to compound a synthesis from a wide variety of sources, materials and experiences. At all costs, they should not constitute the mindless drudgery of copying large chunks from books, because such labours amount to little more than exercises in handwriting.

In conclusion, it must be said that any hierarchy of skills in language and the learning of history is no more than a working hypothesis – a tentative structure for sequential learning. More research is certainly needed in this crucial area; but in broad terms it is fair to say that initial steps in the use of written language will be concerned primarily with the mastery of basic skills, such as vocabulary, thus establishing a necessary foundation for acquiring historical understanding.

ORAL COMMUNICATION

There is general agreement that speaking and listening have immense value as a means to learning[32]. In the words of K. J. Weber:

> The importance of one's speaking ability cannot be overestimated. It is an ability more natural to man than reading or writing. And as a factor in human endeavour, in human development, and in simple day-to-day functioning, the importance of speaking outweighs reading and writing by a considerable margin. Yet so many educators consciously avoid making oral programmes part of a curriculum.[33]

The instinctive quality of oral communication is the key to its importance, particularly for children who may find reading and writing to be initial stumbling blocks to effective learning. Through talking, children can express themselves in language which is familiar and comfortable; discussion also enables children to share ideas and therefore be actively involved in the teaching, as well as the learning, process; and, as Nick Levine points out, discussion can also help in the acquisition of language:

> When students talk they are likely to use their comfortable words, rather than expert language which, in their present state, may confuse rather than clarify; the process of 'talking through' a problem may help to untangle the problem itself but also lead them to understand why and when to use expert language.[34]

It is also clear from examples in the research evidence of Hodgkinson and Long that oral responses from low-achieving children are of a much higher quality than written answers:

> Transcripts of the tape showed longer replies with a more complex sentence structure, much more speculative or probabilistic thinking with inferences made according to external criteria, and more reference to their own background knowledge and application to current events . . . . These examples indicate that pupils could more readily make inferences and judgements, citing evidence, and going beyond the material immediately to hand, when answering orally rather than in written form.[35]

If oral work can be as effective as the research evidence would suggest, then why is it not used more frequently in the teaching of history, especially to the less able? There could be a number of reasons. Writing can ease the difficulties of classroom control by keeping heads down and out of mischief, thus creating a favourable impression to prestigious observers that, through the semblance of order and quietness, effective learning is taking place. The pupils themselves are often unsure with oral work because they lack the necessary social skills to conduct an orderly and meaningful discussion. Indeed, it is not uncommon for children to regard reading and writing as 'real' work, and discussion sessions as something of a soft option or an excuse for wasting time. Moreover, some teachers find difficulty in monitoring the progress of simultaneous discussion groups, which run the risk of following red-herrings and being wasteful, both in terms of time and effort.

   The success of oral work will depend as much on effective lesson planning as the preparation of reading and writing assignments. In particular, the history teacher will need to consider the following: the provision of rich stimuli, which supply the content for discussion; effective questioning techniques and the potential for class discussion; the organisation of small discussion groups; and the appropriate use of mechanical aids. Each of these considerations can be examined in more detail.

1 STIMULI

To be effective, oral work needs a focal point of interest for discussion. There is a rich variety of conventional sources, including extracts from books, primary sources, illustrations, films, and video- and tape-recordings. However, a technique which is emphatically oral in character, and one which has great educational potential, is the use of visitors from the local community[36]. Visitors can range from police liaison officers with a particular interest in the development of the local police force, to members of the local history society and elderly people in the community. Unfortunately, a teacher's efforts can sometimes come to grief when the guest speaker pitches the talk at the wrong level and faces a bored audience of children, or when the children find that they are unable to ask any relevant questions and sustain a conversation with the guest. Such problems can be largely prevented with good pre-planning:

(a) First, the visitor needs to be briefed beforehand with such information as the age and type of children (especially regarding ability), the numbers of children involved (some speakers are very uneasy with large groups), and the main requirements. It is also wise to check beforehand if visitors would have any objections to being recorded on tape or video
(b) Secondly, the children need to be adequately prepared and organised; above all, they must convey the impression to their guest that they are a caring group. Class discussion can focus on such issues as: the preparation of possible questions; who is to make the introductions and how the introductions are to be made; and how the visit is to be concluded gracefully – for example, through a vote of thanks. By preparing an agenda, it is possible to rehearse the event through role-play.

It is important to provide the children with initiative and develop their sense of responsibility. Responding well to visitors can be an aid to the development of social skills as well as tapping a lucrative source of oral history. The visit should create a good lasting impression for both the children and the visitor. It should also provide a foundation for useful follow-up work, especially when the proceedings have been recorded on tape or video.

2 QUESTIONING

A former colleague once told me of an experience very early in his teaching career with a group of low achievers. After an extended monologue about dairy farming, the teacher asked his silent and apparently captivated audience if there were any questions. No response seemed to be forthcoming until a boy at the back of the class raised his hand and said: 'Yeah! D'yer fancy buyin' a ferret?' Questioning of this type serves at least one useful purpose: that of gauging the level of pupil interest through the nature of the response. In this case, it was clear to the teacher that he had rambled on for too long, with the result that the children had totally switched off.

Many, if not most, questions asked in lessons are 'what' questions – that is to say, questions of the closed variety which are limited to factual recall. Such questions are not without value, but there is a danger of emphasising the importance of memory and finding the 'right' answer at the expense of understanding. Indeed, some teachers instantly reject answers which are incorrect, so that the children feel inhibited and reluctant to articulate their doubts with a view to having them resolved.

A more fruitful approach is to concentrate on open, divergent questions, with the objective of achieving what Nick Levine calls a 'learning dialogue'. These 'why' questions are designed to lead the children into imaginative thinking – a thoughtful consideration of probabilities and explanations which transcend what is immediately apparent from the facts. After all, questions such as these are akin to those which historians ask themselves when conducting their own research and writing: questions which take into account evidence, judgement and an element of speculation. Of course, children cannot be expected to make an immediate response to questions of a searching nature. Time should be allowed for them to consider various possibilities – perhaps working in small groups – and to jot them down in writing. It is vitally important for the teacher to value every child's response and to discourage any form of ridicule. As ideas are submitted in answer to the questions, they can be summarised or listed on the blackboard for discussion and clarification. In this way, the children can see that their views are taken seriously, and that they are making a valuable contribution to their own learning process. The teacher will, of course, clear up any misconceptions and draw attention to any omissions which have gone unnoticed by the class.

3 GROUP DISCUSSION

The value of group discussion has been succinctly expressed by the ILEA Inspectorate:

> Small group discussions are another important way of encouraging pupils to develop and examine their own ideas, responses and experiences, and relate these to the views of other people. In this way, they will gain a deeper understanding and wider view of particular issues than each could achieve through individual enquiry.[37]

Moreover, through discussion children are able to use informal language of their own, with the sole purpose of talking through, and sorting out, a problem. Such use of language is refreshingly free of the constraints imposed on so much of the written work that children are expected to produce in school.

The success of discussion work will depend on the development of vital skills of communication. Teachers cannot afford to leave the acquisition of these skills to chance, but set them down as precise objectives in their schemes of work. Preparatory discussion about the value and correct conduct of discussion (supported by various activities and simulations) will establish a useful foundation and hopefully prevent future difficulties, especially in the case of those children unaccustomed to this type of activity[38]. Children need to be aware of at least three essential skills:

(a) Expressing a point of view – the aim being to help others to learn (not showing off); the importance of speaking, even if shy; the importance of eye contact with the group; the need to speak in turn, and not interrupt or shout down others; the value of having a pencil and notepad as an aid to recall.
(b) Listening to the ideas of others – the aim being to learn from the other people (not to ignore or ridicule); the importance of listening to everyone's point of view; how you would feel if others were not willing to listen to your opinions; the value of jottings as an aid to recall.
(c) Responding to the ideas of others – the aim being to sustain the discussion; the value of thinking of questions in response to what has been said; the value of ironing out misconceptions and prejudices, including one's own; that there is no disgrace in admitting to being wrong, or in asking for a point to be explained/clarified; the importance of giving clear reasons for agreeing/disagreeing with what is said, and of drawing the group's attention to a good point which they have too readily dismissed.

Group work also requires careful planning and organisation on the part of the teacher. Each of the following is a serious matter for consideration:

(a) Group size – Small groups of about four pupils are to be preferred. They are easier to manage, they encourage shy children to be more forthcoming, and they ensure that every child has the opportunity to speak.
(b) Selecting a suitable topic – The discussion should be confined to a very specific theme, so that it remains purposeful and avoids being too discursive. The preparation of a sequential agenda of key questions and ideas for discussion can also help to keep the group on course. The choice of topic must be determined by what is familiar to the pupils – perhaps based on the subject content of previous lessons – so that they are sufficiently knowledgeable to make a valuable contribution to the discussion.
(c) Time limitations – Fixing a reasonable time limit will encourage the children to keep to important issues and develop a sense of urgency: that a specific time objective has to be met. Ten minutes' discussion on a specific issue is usually sufficient before reporting back to the whole class.
(d) The allocation of roles and responsibilities – Specific tasks will help the pupils to develop vital skills in communication, as well as assist the efficient running of the group discussion. Each group should have a chairperson; a recorder (to act as a scribe); and a reporter (to report the group's findings to the whole class). Although such responsibilities are better accepted on a voluntary basis, the children should be encouraged to change roles from time to time, in order to widen their experience and build their confidence.
(e) Monitoring progress – The teacher needs to circulate and assess the climate of discussion within each group. Intervention should be carefully and sensitively planned, so that a group in obvious difficulty can be helped forward; for example, if the discussion has drifted off target; if a stage of deadlock has been reached; or if points of detail need expert advice from the teacher.

4 MECHANICAL AIDS

Sound recording is an invaluable artificial aid to the development of linguistic skills and pupil understanding. Several useful machines are now available to teachers, including the synchrofax (or 'talking page') and the language master, both of which work on the important principle of linking sound (the spoken word) with visual display (the written word). James Hagerty and Malcolm Hill provide a very useful discussion on the use of these machines in the teaching of history[39]. Another sequential and programmed learning process is the Phonic Blend Systems (PBS), a comprehensive audio-visual course to develop basic skills in English language. Separate units, used extensively in remedial departments, are commercially available for vocabulary (the 'talking dictionary'), spelling and reading. The pupils are then expected to apply their reading skills and powers of comprehension to stories which utilise the words introduced in the work units. History teachers could initially liaise with remedial teachers and learn something of the principles of the techniques before producing their own tape recordings and accompanying worksheets.

The benefits of using teaching aids which synchronise audio and visual information are considerable:

(a) They are of great benefit to children with specific learning disabilities, including dyslexia, by helping them to overcome problems of aural discrimination.
(b) They enable children to work individually at their own pace (when using earphones), therefore enabling the teacher to circulate and help others.
(c) They can be applied with equal benefit to children working in small groups.
(d) The operation of the machines develops not only linguistic skills but also manual skills, and as such can be an aid to motivation.
(e) The approach is based on the principle of programmed instruction and is therefore conducive to the drawing up of precise educational objectives, in that teachers must work out a programme that is geared towards developing specific linguistic skills and historical concepts.

Whatever the benefits of such mechanical aids – and these are obviously many – it must be emphasised that they can never act as an adequate substitute for the teacher. There will always be children who fail to understand or to concentrate adequately, despite the ingenuity and novelty value of the apparatus employed. Teachers should, therefore, monitor individual progress very carefully and iron out difficulties as and when they occur.

Tape-recorders are more widely available to history departments. Like the machines mentioned above, they can be a useful aid to remediation by linking sound to the written word. When children read their own work into the tape-recorder, the play-back can reveal errors and help the children to correct their own mistakes. However, one of the most valuable functions of the tape-recorder is its potential for building up a library of source material in the form of recorded oral history. Such material is likely to include interviews with old people about local history and past experiences/events of national significance, with the advantage that the conversations are on permanent record, and can be edited, used and re-used in the classroom situation. Moreover, the children themselves can be encouraged to devise questionnaires and record their own interviews on tape. In this way – no matter how elementary – the pupils are actively involved in the process of actually 'doing' history.

In the classroom, the tape-recorder should be a stimulus to inferential thinking; that is to say, the children should be encouraged to develop the habit of raising questions as they listen, and so increase their powers of understanding and retention. When the teacher has studied the content of the tape-recording beforehand, the pupils can have their attention drawn to salient points by such preliminary instructions as:

(a) While you are listening, try to work out what would have happened if such and such had not taken place (skills of prediction/extrapolation).
(b) Decide the point in the story at which. : . . . (skill of analysis).
(c) From the way Mrs. . . . . (the interviewee) speaks about such and such, try to work out if she would have supported. . . . . (skills of comprehension and detection of bias).
(d) Remember what the book said about such and such? See if Mrs. . . . . (the interviewee) agrees from what she says. If not, why not? (appreciation of evidence and the conflict of evidence).

Some of these points can now be illustrated by a case study in the use of a sample tape-recording.

THE TAPE-RECORDER AND ORAL HISTORY: A SAMPLE STUDY

The following transcript is an extract from a recorded interview with Miss Doris Raynor on her seventy-ninth birthday (6th April 1983). Questions focused on Doris's working life in Leeds earlier this century and the working lives of her relatives, particularly her late mother (1860–1953). The purpose of the interview was to provide source material for children following a course in social history. Of course, a written transcript can never do justice to the actual sound recording, which transmits all the subtleties of voice inflexion and intonation and Doris's ebullient sense of humour – qualities which help to make Doris a story-teller *par excellence*. However, the content of the transcript gives something of the flavour of the interview and its potential as a teaching resource.

Q. How old were you, Doris, when you left school?

A. Thirteen.

Q. And where did you go then?

A. Mellish's: we had to start at six o'clock, till half past five. That was a big leap, wasn't it? And there was the Commissionnaire at the door with his medals on; and if you weren't to the minute, you got locked out and you had to stop there till breakfast time. It was like that, oh yes. Oh, it belonged Mellish's then; now it belongs Lodge's – do you see?

Q. What kind of work was done in Mellish's?

A. Everything: dyeing, weaving, spinning and piecening and mending – everything; it's a complete mill.

Q. This was a woollen mill, was it?

A. Woollen and worsted.

Q. Did you enjoy working there?

A. I was only there two days (chuckle). When I told my mother, she played 'hummer' with me – that I'd gone into the mill, because she was a weaver, you see. And I went and found my own job while my mother was working. I was a go-getter, you know!

Q. So why did you leave after just two days?

A. Well, my mother played 'hummer' with me – she did. She threatened me. (chuckle)

Q. So why didn't your mum want you to work at Mellish's?

A. Well, she didn't want me to work in the mill at all – she really didn't. She knew I wasn't strong. But any road, I've lived to be 79 haven't I? (chuckle) Isn't it wonderful? And Dr Robertson said to me when I lived at Whingate: 'Do you know, Miss Raynor – my father: he'd have been astonished had he been living: we never thought you'd live beyond your thirteenth birthday.' I was so delicate; but I'm here yet. And my mother: she lived to be 93 and she was delicate in her youth.

Q. Your mother had a hard life, didn't she, Doris?

A. Oh yes – very hard. I was born in lodgings, you know: anybody had to look after me.

Q. Did your mother work in the mill at this time?

A. Oh yes. You see, when one place went slack they used to have to go to another one to find work. It was difficult, even in them days, to get a job, you know. And do you know what they did? As soon as I was born, they (the neighbours) came to see me. . . . . and they said to my mother: 'What are you going to call her?' She said: 'Call her One-t'-many.' (chuckle) When my mother told me that, I laughed my hat off (chuckle). But One-t'-many turned out to look after her in her old age when she had a stroke. That's really what's wrong with my back now – with lifting.

Q. This was lifting you did in the mill, was it, Doris?

A. Lifting my mother – and I had a lot of lifting in the mill.

Q. When you left Mellish's after two days, where did you go to work then?

A. Oh, I put my foot in it again: I went to Roberts', and it was asbestos. And they had a place in Eyres' mill, if you remember, where Lodge's is – opposite Armley Park. I didn't know it was dangerous; nobody said ought to us. Well, I had to go to the doctor's, so I had to leave there.

Q. Can you remember any cases of people suffering from work: diseases and injuries – that kind of thing?

A. Oh, I've seen a few felled wi' shuttle: they go down like a poleaxe. They fly out if a thread gets in.

Q. What kind of wages were people paid in those days?

A. Oh, when the flu was about, and my mother thought, 'Well, she isn't strong', and thought, 'I'll send her away to service, so she'll be out of the way of all the germs.' And, do you know, all I had was five shillings a week – for a full day from 7 till 10 o'clock at night, seven days a week. And we only had half a day off, and we'd to start washing up and be in at nine.

Q. Was this about the time when the First World War came to an end?

A. Yes, you're right. They were shouting about 'Specials'. 'Read all about it!' And they sent me out, and the war was over.

Q. What were the 'Specials'?

A. It was about the war: the First World War – when it was over: 'Read all about it!' – do you see? And they were running from one street to another. . . . . . And I'll tell you what: (in) those days, before you could be poorly, or have a baby, or ought like that, you had to have a substitute weaver, do you see? Now my mother went as a substitute to Mellish's for a month, then she went to Fox's (that's where the Imperial Laundry is) and she'd to walk every foot o' the road – there and back. I don't know how they did it; life was hard.

Q. How many children had your mother to look after, Doris?

A. I've five brothers and a sister – I had, anyway. My last brother was 86 when he died; and it's two years since he died.

Q. So your mother was looking after a large family and working in the mill at the same time?

A. Well, you see, men had poor wages then; they only got a pound – a guinea – a week. It was very difficult, you know. And how they went on when it was holidays – Easter, Whitsuntide Bank Holiday and Christmas – I don't know what they did, I really don't know. Do you know, I've thought about it many a time, I really have. And do you know, my sister once said to me: 'Do you know, Doris, I've seen my mother eat no end of dry bread so we could have it.' It was so bad.

Q. What do you think the trade union leaders would say about that today?

A. Well, you know, they'd have a shock. And I'll tell you another thing. Now then: my mother was born at Old Farnley, and my grandfather was a butler at Farnley Hall, you see. And he'd seven sons and my mother. And they were all round the bed, and he died when he was 44 – he'd got pneumonia, and they didn't know he'd been working with it. Well, being a farmer's daughter, she knew what to do; so they'd pigs and hens and all that sort of thing. And, do you know, my youngest uncle: they carried young ones on their backs did older ones, and he was only 7 years old, and they did a twelve-hour shift in the mine – in the drift mine – and they had candles, and they were coloured – I've seen them – and when they got to a certain colour (blue and green and all them) they knew they'd done an hour; do you see? It was marvellous, you know, but it was very . . . well, it could have blown up, couldn't it?

Q. Where was this mine where your grandfather worked?

A. It was at the bottom of Tong – this drift mine. No, it wasn't my grandfather; it was his son. And older ones had to carry younger ones on their backs. My last uncle was only 7 years old.

Q. Was this because the children were so tired?

A. Well, they had to be up early, hadn't they? And they had to walk every foot o' the way; there was no riding in them days. You go in the bus now to Farnley. Well, there was nothing like that – no! And there were no lamps. My mother worked at Troydale at one time when she was younger, and it was pitch black – and they had to take off at 5 to get there for 6. And to come up there: Oh, my goodness! I don't know how she did it.

Q. And she'd get back home at about half past six, would it be?

A. Yes – eh, she was fair done. She worked at Troydale (mill) during the time that I was going to be born.

The tape-recording stimulated interest in low achievers of various ages, ranging from second to fifth year (12 to 16 years). Not only is the subject content related to social themes which are concrete and familiar, but the use of language is simple and expressive – even colloquial in character – and readily comprehensible. Discussion, both before and after hearing the tape recording, was aimed at stimulating inferential thinking in the children. Their attention was drawn to a number of important issues:

(a) Aspects of social life, including: working conditions (e.g. hours of work, wages, sickness and injury); the position of women (family responsibilities and the need to work); and the treatment of children.

(b) Evidence – The children were asked to think carefully about Doris's claim that her uncle worked down a drift mine at 7 years of age (he was close in age to Doris's mother, who was born in 1860), using coloured candles. The children were reminded of the Mines Act of 1842 (which prohibited the employment of children below ground if they were under 10 years old) and the invention of the Davy safety lamp in 1815, which was intended to replace candles.

The written work produced by the children varied in quality. Gavin's attempt to write a short account of Doris's working life was conscientiously done, but relies almost exclusively on facts, with little or no attempt to express an opinion or to pass judgement on the circumstances (Fig. 4.3). On the other hand, Janet's design of a questionnaire (for use with her great-grandmother) shows application and creative thinking (Fig. 4.4). Both Gavin and Janet are aged 13 and members of a small withdrawal class with learning difficulties.

In general, the discussion work was more interesting and speculative. In conversation, the children were certainly capable of giving serious considera-

Fig. 4.3 A Sample of Work by Gavin

19/1/84   Dorries

Dorries left School at 13 years and stared work at a Mill and which it was in leeds. When she started the time was 6·30 and and finished at 6·30pm. She had to walk 2 miles to get to work She was born in leejings She got pay 5 shillings and at the end of the week. She earned 25 Shillings at work. She was weving People under 7 years of age. they could not work. only over 10 years of age you could work they worked under mines. they used candles they had stripes if one stripe went down it would. be 1 hour.

tion to the conflict of evidence between what was said by Doris and what we understand from the textbooks. This is indicated in the following short extract from a small group discussion of low achievers in their fifth year:

Peter: I reckon Doris is right – she lived then and should know what she's talking about. Books are like newspapers: you can't believe what they say.

Teacher: Yes – a very good point, Peter. I wondered if Doris had meant that her grandfather had worked down the mine at the age of 7, but she was very certain that it was her uncle. On the other hand, I'm sure that the books are right about the Mines Act; the facts are easy to check from records. What if the books are right and Doris is right. Can you think of any other possible explanation?

Sandra: Just because there are laws it doesn't mean that they won't be broken. Laws are being broken all the time.

Tony: And people were that badly off then they were starving. They would do anything. They just had to work.

Teacher: Yes – I'm sure you are right about the law being broken; and parents who were desperate for money would probably send their children to work, although they were under age. Why was it easy to break the law?

Fig. 4.4   A Sample of Work by Janet

Working in Mills

1. What age did you Start work.
2. How many hours did you work a day.
3. What Kind of work did you do.
4. Did you have any children when you were working.
5. What Kind of meal did you have for dinner.
6. What Kind of cloths did you wear for work.
7. How much wages did you get.
8. How far did you have to walk to work
9. What age did you get marriaged.
10. Did you give your mum all your wages.

The discussion developed from there about such issues as the reasons for the evasion of the law and the problem of bias in writing and reporting (Peter's original point), which was worthy of discussion in its own right. Inferential or exploratory thinking of this kind was certainly not as evident in written work. This was partly due to the fact the children found written expression more difficult, and partly due to the stimulus of group dynamics on the cultivation and expression of ideas.

CONCLUSION

Language development is vitally important to the teaching and understanding of history. However, language is not always the 'enabling factor in learning'; it sometimes creates barriers to communication and understanding: the problems, particularly for low achievers, are many and varied. It is important for history teachers to share the responsibility for establishing basic linguistic skills as a foundation for those skills and concepts which are clearly historical in nature. The teaching of many basic skills, including vocabulary, lends itself to the objectives approach, the use of programmed learning and various mechanical aids. Liaison and co-ordination with remedial specialists in devising foundation schemes to help the child with language disabilities can be invaluable.

Attention needs to be drawn not only to the way language is presented to low achievers, through curricular materials and teacher exposition, but also to the demands placed on pupils in their own use of language. Written work has a vital role to play, and should be developed sequentially, but oral communication is of equal significance. Indeed, in some ways, such as an interchange of ideas through discussion, it is unquestionably superior. Sadly, oral skills have been neglected in many schools, so that low achievers frequently lack the necessary social skills to conduct an orderly and beneficial discussion. Where this problem exists, it should be tackled; but the enterprising teacher will need patience: the patience to introduce new approaches very gradually and the will to persevere if discussion lessons are not an instant success.

I should like to conclude with the observations of John Slater, HMI, who, at the conference of the Historical Association in London on the 10th February 1984, stated:

> HMI sees an increasing number of history teachers who now realise that more attention must be given to the accessibility of the language of history teaching – the language that is used in talking to pupils, of examination questions and the language in the books that they read . . . If the language becomes more accessible, you can correspondingly increase the demand of the intellectual task. Some of the most exciting work that we have seen in schools is from lower achieving pupils using primary source material and thinking in a way that most of us would regard as genuinely historical.

REFERENCES

1 W. Burston, *Principles of history teaching*. Methuen, 1963, p. 49
2 J. Coltham, *The development of thinking and the learning of history*. Historical Association, 1971, p. 24
3 D. G. Watts, *The learning of history*. Routledge & Kegan Paul, 1972, p. 26
4 Bullock Report, *A language for life*. HMSO, 1975, para. 133
5 M. Marland, *Language across the curriculum*. Heinemann, 1977, p. 3
6 B. D. Roe et al, *Reading instruction in the secondary school*. Rand McNally, 1978, p. 221
7 A. D. Edwards, 'The language of history and the communication of historical knowledge'. In A. K. Dickinson and P. J. Lee (eds.), *History teaching and historical understanding*. Heinemann, 1978, p. 65
8 Quoted in G. Bernbaum, 'Language and history teaching'. In W. Burston and C. Green (eds.), *Handbook for history teachers*. Methuen, 1972, p. 40
9 This important distinction is emphasised in J. D. Nichol, 'The teaching of history 11–18: a consistent approach'. *Teaching history*, 25, 1979
10 H. Allen, 'Local history studies for slow-learning children'. In V. McIver (ed.), *Teaching history to slow-learning children in secondary schools*. Belfast, 1982, pp. 117–121
11 See C. Harrison, *Readability in the classroom*. Cambridge University Press, 1980, pp. 128–131; E. Lunzer and K. Gardner (eds.), *The effective use of reading*. Heinemann, 1979, p. 85
12 C. Harrison, *op. cit.*, pp. 51–81; V. McIver (ed.), *op. cit.*, pp. 45, 54–56; M. Hinson (ed.), *Encouraging results*. Macdonald, 1978, pp. 118–119, 231; Open University Reading Development Course PE 261, units 8 and 9, 1973
13 T. Arkel, 'How well do readability tests detect difficulties in history texts?'. *Teaching history*, 32, 1982, p. 25.
14 W. Kintsch, *The representation of meaning in memory*. Hillsdale, N.J., 1974
15 Quoted in C. Harrison, *op. cit.*, p. 131
16 N. Levine, *Language, teaching and learning: history*. Ward Lock, 1981, pp. 86–88
17 *Ibid.*, p. 88
18 T. Arkel, *op. cit.*, p. 25
19 C. Harrison, *op. cit.*, p. 130
20 A. Stokes, 'The reliability of readability formulae'. *Journal of Research in Reading*, vol. 1, 1978, pp. 21–34; T. Arkel, *op. cit.*, p. 25
21 C. Harrison, *op. cit.*, pp. 140–141
22 M. Hinson (ed.), *op. cit.*, p. 119
23 J. Coltham, *op. cit.*, p. 22
24 D. P. Ausubel and F. G. Robinson, *School learning: an introduction to educational psychology*. Holt, Rinehart & Winston, 1969, p. 145
25 E. A. Peel, 'Some problems in the psychology of history teaching'. In W. Burston and D. Thompson (eds.), *Studies in the nature and teaching of history*. Routledge & Kegan Paul, 1967, p. 173
26 N. Martin et al, *Writing and learning across the curriculum 11–16*. Ward Lock, 1976
27 J. Hull, 'Practical points on teaching history to less able secondary pupils'. *Teaching History*, 28, 1980, p. 23
28 R. Binns, 'A technique for developing written language'. In M. M. Clark and T. Glynn (eds.), *Reading and writing for the child with difficulties*. Educational Review Occasional Publication no. 8, 1980
29 M. D. Wilson, 'Teaching history to slow learners: problems of language and communication.' *Teaching History*, 33, 1982, pp. 23–25
30 See, for example, V. McIver (ed.), *op. cit.*, pp. 72–84, 89–105; J. Hull, *op. cit.*; D.

Griffin, *Slow learners: a break in the circle.* Woburn, 1978, pp. 163–165; E. Cowie, *History and the slow-learning child.* Historical Association, 1979; K. Hodgkinson and M. Long, 'The assassination of John F. Kennedy – a skills-based approach for remedial pupils'. *Teaching History.* 29, 1981

31 J. Hull, *op. cit.*, p. 21
32 See, for example, E. Lunzer and K. Gardner, *op. cit.*, pp. 17–24; N. Levine, *op. cit.* pp. 106–110; K. Hodgkinson and M. Long, *op. cit*
33 K. J. Weber, *Yes, they can: a practical guide for teaching the adolescent slow learner.* Open University Press, 1978, p. 51
34 N. Levine, *op. cit.*, pp. 107–108
35 K. Hodgkinson and M. Long, *op. cit.*, p. 6
36 See, for example, S. Purkis, 'An experiment in family history with first year juniors'. *Teaching history*, vol. IV, 1975, pp. 250–256
37 ILEA, *History and social sciences at secondary level – Part Two: History*, 1982, p. 50
38 For some useful guidelines, see, for example, D. Gunning, *The teaching of history.* Croom Helm, 1978, pp. 71–73, 84–85; L. Button, *Group tutoring for the form teacher.* Books 1 & 2. Hodder & Stoughton, 1982/3; L. Button, *Developmental group work with adolescents.* Hodder & Stoughton, 1975; D. Hamblin, *Teaching study skills.* Basil Blackwell, 1981; M. Marland, *op. cit.*, pp. 129–137
39 J. Hagerty and M. Hill, 'History and less able children'. *Teaching History*, 30, 1981, pp. 19–22
40 J. Slater, 'The case for history in school'. *The Historian*, 2, 1984, p. 15

5

Concrete Aids to Learning

INTRODUCTION

Piaget's research on the stages of cognitive growth has deservedly received widespread acclaim and acceptance in educational literature, for, above all, it emphasises the fact that the thought processes of children differ qualitatively from those of adults. In accordance with Piagetian theory, the thinking of children in the stage of 'concrete operations' (most primary children and many low achievers in the secondary school) is largely limited to concrete, descriptive responses which are tied to the immediate circumstantial details of the material presented for study. Although Piaget's work, particularly in its application to historical education, has been subjected to increasing criticism, it underlines the importance of conveying the structure of a subject discipline in a form which is readily comprehensible to children; in other words, appropriate to the child's stage of cognitive development. Indeed, if this is accomplished, according to Bruner, it should be possible that 'any subject can be taught in some intellectually honest form to any child at any stage of development.'[1]

Bruner distinguishes three 'modes of representation': the enactive (learning by doing), the iconic (learning from seeing) and the symbolic (learning through the use of conventional symbols of language):

> We can talk of three ways in which somebody 'knows' something – through doing it, through a picture or image of it, and through some such symbolic means as language.[2]

These modes are not meant to be age bound, but interact and are inter-dependent at every stage of a child's education. Nevertheless, the concrete representations of the subject are clearly associated with the enactive and iconic modes: those which are the most tangible, immediate and familiar. They are akin to what Thomson terms 'primary perception', which is gained from first-hand experience, as opposed to 'secondary perception', which is acquired second-hand from reading and instruction[3]. In the widest possible sense, concrete associations must encompass both the choice of subject content and the nature of the language employed in the teaching and learning process. Terry Langman, for example, argues very convincingly that one of the best ways of introducing history to low achievers is through family history, because it proceeds from 'the known': relatives and family mementoes are palpable and immediate associations[4]. Similarly, Nick Levine uses the term 'concrete language' to describe communication which is both natural and 'comfortable' for the children to use as a means of expression[5]. However, syllabus content and language and communication have been discussed at length in earlier chapters, so the emphasis in this chapter will be on activity-based learning and the visual dimension in the teaching and study of history.

First, there is need for a word of caution. It would be folly to suggest that the visual dimension is inevitably more straight-forward for the child with learning difficulties, or that activity-based learning (such as model-making) necessarily accelerates historical understanding. Historical sites and archaeological ruins can be extremely demanding source materials; and visual evidence in the form of contemporary prints, caricatures and cartoons is frequently imbued with propaganda, bias and other such subtleties, which can be extremely difficult for the low achiever to grasp. Clearly, the appropriate use of such material will require more than a *prima facie* interpretation, and the teacher must exercise care and discretion in the selection of visual material for use with the less able. In the words of Lowe:

> The myth which haunts history teaching, that visual evidence is necessarily simpler than documentary, must be dispelled once and for all.[6]

These reservations have been justified by recent research findings. It is frequently assumed, for example, that field courses are an invaluable visual aid for young and low achieving children because they can learn from the primary experience of direct observation. However, this assumption has been seriously questioned by Pond on the basis of an experimental study of field work with seventy-four middle-school children of mixed ability and aged 8 to 12 years. Test results revealed very clearly that it was the most able pupils who benefited from visits because they were better able to perceive the past from evidence that survives and to express an empathetic response. Thus Pond cast doubt on the claim that school visits are particularly useful as an aid to understanding for children at the stage of concrete operations, and emphasised the fact that teachers cannot afford to assume that children have understood simply because they have seen.

One of the major educational problems highlighted by this research arises from the very nature of history as a subject discipline. The past cannot be concrete in any real sense because it cannot be directly observed. What *is* seen through field work is, in fact, a residual of the past, such as an artefact or an ancient ruin; and an understanding of history can only be achieved by using these 'residuals' as pieces of concrete evidence for an imaginative reconstruction of the past. This requires a process of thinking which is both mature and highly sophisticated. An unwise choice of visit can, therefore, be a source of confusion to children of low ability, because they are likely to have difficulty in distinguishing (on the basis of observation) between 'what is' and 'what was'. In the words of M. Pond, there is a danger that some pupils 'will be seduced by what is immediately sensibly perceptible and will ignore the historical experience from which they are separated by the passage of time.'[7]

Similar reservations have been expressed about the efficacy of the so-called 'activity' methods in history teaching. Various forms of art work and model-making, for example, have been strongly recommended by a number of writers, especially in the context of primary education, with many useful practical hints on how such work can be successfully implemented in the classroom[8]. They argue that such work is imaginative and creative; fosters group activity, co-operation and communication; develops a wide range of artistic and practical skills; and motivates children with language problems by providing an alternative means of expression to reading and writing. Of course, there can be considerable value in activity of this kind, especially where the children are expected to work from historical sources to ensure that their models are reasonably authentic, and where children are required to interpret and explain the nature of their work in historical terms. However, there can be significant problems, particularly in the secondary school. Many history teachers, for example, lack the necessary training to do first class art and craft work, and will almost certainly need to liaise closely with the art/craft departments. They are also likely to lack specialist rooms and storage space for all the necessary paraphernalia; and, should all this be made available, single (or even double) periods would hardly seem to justify the inevitable wrangle in preparation and clearing up. There is always a danger, too, that older pupils will find this type of work childish, not to say patronising. But, above all, we must honestly answer the question: is it really history? In the words of Dr P. J. Rogers:

> Frequently the new 'activity' approach is not practised upon, or disciplined by, genuine evidence, and, consequently, is not shaped by its proper use. All too often, little genuine evidence is presented (in which case the reconstruction becomes mere imaginative composition, or art, or handwork, without any basis in fact) or it is presented uncritically, not as something out of which a narrative or picture or model can be constructed by inference, cross-referencing and so on, but as a substitute for any such operations.[9]

In accordance with Bruner's 'spiral curriculum' (see Chapter 1), it should first be necessary for children to acquire the more concrete *percepts* and simpler conceptual experiences before proceeding to the more abstract and comprehensive representations of the subject. The immediacy of visual and practical experience can obviously be a very potent force in this respect. However, concrete representations of this kind should not only motivate the child, but also be appropriate to the child's stage of mental development, and, as M. Pond's research has shown, this is not the case. Observation and practical work should also contribute to concept formation and historical understanding through the process of 'translation': that is to say, the visual or practical experience must 'carry the message' which it is intended to convey – some form of understanding of the past. Sadly, many illustrations are not used as concrete evidence and fail to contribute significantly to the development of children's historical thinking.[10]

We can now examine in more detail the educational potential of the visual dimension and activity-based learning in the teaching of history to children with learning difficulties. Each can be discussed in turn.

THE VISUAL DIMENSION

The iconic mode – learning through visual imagery – is both an abused and under-rated medium of instruction. All too often audio-visual aids serve no other purpose than a charitable provision for the less able – a palliative in place of the apparently more intellectually strenuous activities of reading and writing. In the words of Evelyn Cowie:

> Whilst history pictures can stimulate the imagination and bring understanding of the past, they can only contribute to the pupil's knowledge if they are actively used. Too often they seem to be decoration on the wall or in the textbook.[11]

It is also a pity that many of the best audio-visual aids on history, including films and television documentaries, have not been produced with low achievers in mind: the visual impact is frequently offset by a complex commentary. It is vitally important that teachers make a judicious selection of visual material. With respect to films, there are basically two types available: the archive film or newsreel, which can be used as a primary source, and the feature film (including short study extracts), which is less authentic, but often simpler to understand and more dramatic in effect. A number of specialist articles provide both valuable advice and copious lists of available films and film distributors[12]. Consulting these is to be strongly recommended before sending off any orders, either for hire or for purchase. Difficulties can also be minimised if teachers are able to view the films or programmes first and draw their pupils' attention to salient features beforehand. These points can then be reinforced afterwards through class discussion and the keeping of some record. Similarly, in the use of slides and filmstrips teachers should take into account the children's limited powers of concentration and retention. It is, therefore, far more effective to show a limited number of slide frames, which can be observed and discussed in some detail.

In spite of the problems outlined above, the potential value of pictures and visual imagery has long been realised. In the summer of 1932, for example, Professor H. Johnson spent six weeks in New York teaching American history through motion pictures to high school students in their seventh grade. Each film lasted about fifteen minutes, followed by thirty-five minutes of discussion. The children were asked to write a report about their 'picture lessons', and 'without exception these reports compared "picture lessons" with textbook lessons greatly to the disadvantage of the latter.'[13] Johnson's conclusions are as relevant to history teachers today as they were when they were first voiced over forty years ago:

> School history, to be made real and kept real, should begin with realities which can either be observed directly or which can be represented directly, and should

continue throughout the school course to provide frequent opportunities for appeals to such materials. . . . History throughout the elementary course should abound in concrete details for visualizing persons, situations, events. In meeting this condition even trivialities are permissible. Facts spurned by the standard historians may furnish the very touch needed to make the misty immortals of history really human.[14]

The importance of visual material can be defended both in terms of the process of education and in the procedure of historical enquiry. Psychological research has indicated that learning through seeing is an integral part of the cognitive processes in building mental images; storing experiences, ideas and concepts; and assisting in creative expression and problem-solving.[15] According to C. E. Wilkinson, people also retain more knowledge as a result of observation, test results indicating nine per cent from reading, eighteen per cent from listening, and twenty-seven per cent from seeing[16]. Moreover, the great strides made in reprographic and media technology in recent years have provided history teachers with opportunities which at one time were hardly dreamed of. In the words of Dr R. Unwin:

> For the history teacher it is becoming a matter of some urgency that more attention should be given to the problems and the possibilities of visual sources. At a time when visual information is proliferating so rapidly, it is hardly surprising that terms such as 'visual literacy' and 'graphicacy' are being used increasingly in all fields of education.[17]

The implication is obvious: children need to be taught in the use of visual evidence just as they do in the use of the written word.

There is also a growing recognition of the importance of visual evidence among professional historians, especially with regard to twentieth-century source materials, such as archive film and contemporary photographs; but it must be stressed that many rich and varied sources of visual evidence are available for earlier periods too[18]. The use of such evidence with children (of all abilities) in the classroom has proved a successful way of encouraging historical thinking. Dr M. B. Booth's longitudinal study of fifty-three pupils (aged fifteen plus) underlined the importance of visual stimuli in promoting this:

> The oral testing of the nature and structure of the pupils' historical thinking showed that seventy-one per cent were able to draw two or more pieces of pictorial evidence into a connected, imaginative synthesis; that they could go beyond the surface impression and infer qualities or ideas. They found it more difficult to use the quotations in this way but even so fifty-eight per cent were able to form sets of two or more pieces of evidence.[19]

Furthermore, a pilot study of children's questions in history by A. C. Brown indicates the potential value of pictorial evidence. A mixed-ability group (aged 13:11 to 14:8) were presented with an authentic propaganda war poster from the period 1940–41 (borrowed through the Museum Loan Service) and asked to list their own impressions and questions for discussion. The poster made a visual impact and stimulated creative, divergent thinking. Brown presents a convincing argument for allowing pupils greater scope for developing their own insights, and for a greater utilisation of pupils' own ideas and observations in the study and teaching of history.[20]

As an aid to teaching history, visual representation serves four major functions.

1 EVIDENCE

Old photographs, prints and other contemporary illustrations can provide vivid source material and evidence in concrete terms that low achievers are able to appreciate and understand. When carefully selected, such illustrations can also arouse an empathetic response. As John Hull points out:

> The history teacher can foster the valid skill of accurate observation and through pictures can introduce a wealth of primary source material which is within the ability of less able children to handle.[21]

Hull provides an interesting example of a worksheet on nineteenth-century mining conditions based on reproductions of the illustrations in the various parliamentary papers. An example of my own, showing a Victorian street scene in Wigan, is shown in Appendix C. Pictures such as this provide striking evidence of continuity and change within the locality, especially when the places are visited and directly observed with a view to contrasting 'then' and 'now'. Reference has already been made to the subtleties of many contemporary cartoons and caricatures, but this is intended as a caveat, not an argument against their use; it is, after all, important that pupils gain some insight into the concepts of bias and propaganda, and become aware of the manipulation and distortion of public opinion through the media. Perhaps a useful starting point is to choose a topic of current interest and controversy, and collect cartoons and caricatures from newspapers of all shades of political opinion for the purpose of discussion and analysis.

Primary source material (including facsimiles) can be obtained from local libraries, record offices and museums. Many have education officers attached and some have produced local source packs for use in schools. Teachers' centres have also been active in pooling resources and providing facilities for reproduction and distribution. Moreover, the numerous archive teaching units, including the *Jackdaws* (Jonathan Cape) and the packs produced by various university departments, provide yet another source of invaluable material.[22] Of course, tracing such sources demands time, effort and commitment, and many teachers lack confidence in the use of primary sources, especially with the less able. It is for this reason that the incorporation of pictorial evidence into some recently published textbooks is a most welcome development. Teachers, for example, will find the *Openings in History*[23] series (edited by Dr R. Unwin and published by Hutchinson) both a useful course text and a valuable source of pictorial material, which is an integral part of the proposed lesson format. Teachers should find the series of considerable help in the teaching of younger (lower secondary) and less able children.

An extension of the iconic mode, and the principle of using pictorial evidence, is the use of field trips and museums. A wise choice of visit can provide pupils with a concrete sense of reality with the added advantage of three-dimensional imagery. The Schools Museum Services offer much in the way of advice, worksheets, displays and even replicas for children to handle[24]. This, together with material collected by the children themselves, such as family photographs and 'Victoriana', can provide fruitful resource material for project work.

A number of published articles provide excellent guidelines for teachers planning field work with less able pupils, and are testimony to the fact that such work can be extremely successful. Harry Allen, for example, describes a history trail in a small part of Dungannon which served as the nucleus of a wide range of activities with low achieving pupils, ranging from the completion of a trial booklet to practical activities, such as taking rubbings from old gravestones, measuring railway arches and interviewing local residents on tape. Careful planning with regard to both preparatory and follow-up work is stressed, including the use of local large-scale maps (e.g. six inches to the mile) and slide pictures of local features that should be expected and looked for on the trail. Allen is in no doubt as to the value of such an exercise:

> For the vast majority of those pupils who followed it, the trail more than succeeded in its design. The pupils were able to produce a great amount of wall display material and written work. In one term the pupils not only added a good deal to their historical skills, but learned much about their home town and some of its history. That they should be as interested and absorbed by their work is in no small measure due to the use of the history trail.[25]

In a stimulating article, Andy Reid discusses the use of two activities – surveying and fieldwalking – with mixed-ability pupils of secondary age, thus utilising archaeology in the cause of history teaching. Once again, careful planning and preparation are emphasised as essential, including gaining the support of professional archaeologists, the permission and goodwill of local landowners, and the judicious selection of local sites, ensuring that the chances of a useful find are good and that a sense of worthwhile achievement is guaranteed. Observational and practical skills in the field (e.g. the identification of finds, field sketching and measuring) are followed by equally important work in the classroom, including the writing of reports and the drawing of diagrams, charts and neat copies of sketches, as well as analytical work, such as the mapping of the finds (distribution plans) and attempts at reconstructing the social life of the settlements on the basis of the evidence collected (e.g. prehistoric flint tools and Roman pottery). Such work is organised on a co-operative basis, tasks being related to the ability and aptitude of individuals. In the words of Reid:

> The excitement of finding evidence in the field can motivate and fire the imaginations of pupils of all abilities, as well as leading them to a greater understanding of, in the well-worn phrase, 'what evidence is and what it will prove.' It is evidence which is direct and tangible, posing questions to which all can respond and which can 'stretch' the most able and the least able alike.[26]

2 RECONSTRUCTION

Many illustrations in history textbooks and wallcharts are modern artistic impressions: attempts to depict or reconstruct past events, people and physical remains, such as medieval castles and Viking longships. Much of this material is unhistorical and of limited educational value. First, it can be argued that artists' impressions are rarely authentic; they are often redrawings of contemporary sources and are therefore prone to some degree of falsification. Now that it is much easier to reproduce contemporary prints, engravings and drawings for commercial purposes, their use is to be recommended in preference to second-hand illustrations. After all, contemporary illustrations are representations of how people saw things at the time – that is to say, genuine sources of pictorial evidence. Secondly, artistic reconstructions can be extremely misleading in depicting human actions and emotions. More often than not, they are better described as flights of fancy than as facts of history. In the words of Marjorie Reeves:

> No one knows how King John looked as he faced his barons at Runnymede, yet we have seen many pictures of a scowling John and a pictorial impression makes an even more powerful impact than a fanciful word-description. Some illustrators for educational publishers do not even do their home-work properly: I recently saw an Anglo-Saxon feast depicted in which the feasters used forks![27]

Visual reconstruction can, and should, be governed by the evidence available. Line drawings, for example, can be painstakingly researched to ensure accuracy; and the reconstructed models displayed in museums can be made from genuine materials, and to precise specifications, in order to ensure authenticity. Presentations of this quality are, to use Professor Hexter's terminology, a 'second record' just as viable as the reconstruction of the past expressed in writing, with the likelihood of captivating pupil interest and attention through the immediacy of the visual impact. Unfortunately, however, many commercial illustrations presented to children are both crude and inaccurate, serving no educational purpose, except to say:

> Even where the artistic work is historically faulty, the teacher can often get something of value out of pictures by asking the class to spot an anachronism, criticize a misleading historical impression, or identify the bias in a picture.[28]

Visual reconstruction, as a creative and imaginative process, is perhaps best employed as a means of expression for the children: given the historical ingredients (a story, a quotation, or details about buildings, events or clothes, etc.) the pupils can then be asked to make their own imaginary pictures. Indeed, D. G. Watts argues that the 'associative' element in historical thinking (akin to creativity, imagination and divergent thinking – and including visual imagery) is vitally important in providing the *pseudo-concepts*, from which genuine conceptual understanding (including 'rational' or logical thinking) can be developed[29]. This, of course, is consistent with the implications of Bruner's 'spiral curriculum', discussed earlier.

There is research evidence to suggest the validity of Watts' thesis. W. H.

Nicholls conducted an experiment with a sample of twenty-two adolescent boys in an Adelaide secondary school. All were of low academic ability (the least able twenty per cent of the school population) and their average age was 14:6. The boys were taught about the rise of the USA and the USSR from the use of documents, graphic secondary sources and drama: deliberate attempts to develop associative thinking. They were presented with a series of written statements (e.g. 'While serfs scratched for a living, nobles ate the choicest foods') and asked to express/interpret them, both in visual form (e.g. through the drawing of cartoons) and in writing. The visual interpretations were clearly more interesting, imaginative and insightful than the written answers, indicating a greater number of associations and greater associative strength. Nicholls concluded that the abstract, technical demands of written language (e.g. punctuation, grammar and vocabulary) 'come between the student and the associative process, thus acting as inhibitors.'[30]

Figures 5.1 and 5.2 illustrate Nicholls' point. Both are visual reconstructions of the Black Death by 'withdrawal' pupils of low general ability in their second year (aged 12–13). Having studied the Black Death as part of their history course, the pupils were asked to draw their impressions of the event. No copying was allowed; all the pictures had to be drawn from memory and/or imagination. The first figure (by Tony) is easy to follow and indicates a talent for drawing that would compare with children of much higher academic ability. For Tony, drawing was a comfortable medium of expression, an enjoyable exercise and a means of gaining a real sense of achievement. The second illustration (by Gavin) is *prima facie* less successful: the childlike drawings and the lack of visual perspective are more typical of a child several years younger. But closer inspection reveals a good level of understanding and a degree of sophistication which is not readily apparent. The first frame depicts a scene prior to the outbreak of plague: refuse is being thrown out of a bedroom window, and rats are rummaging through this in the street below. (Notice also the timber framework of the medieval building.) The second frame shows bodies being carted off for burial, with a coffin in the foreground – according to Gavin a 'symbol of death'. The third frame depicts the front door of an afflicted household, the residents warning visitors to 'keep away'; and the final frame is a portrait of a diseased person (complete with buboes and rashes) desperately crying out for help. This is clearly an empathetic response.

Thus pictorial reconstruction can be a creative process and a means of expressing ideas that for some less able pupils would be difficult – not to say impossible – through the highly symbolic medium of written language. It also has the advantage that the pupils are fully aware that the work is a product of their *own* imaginations – history not necessarily as it was, but as they think it was. This subtle distinction between fact and interpretation is less clear when children are presented with visual material which is the product of the imaginations of others, including the illustrators of modern textbooks.

Fig. 5.1   Visual Impressions of the Black Death by Tony (aged 13)

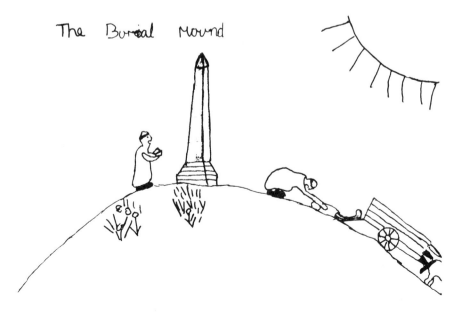

The horse and cart Carrying the Dead body's to the Burial Mount

The Burial Mound

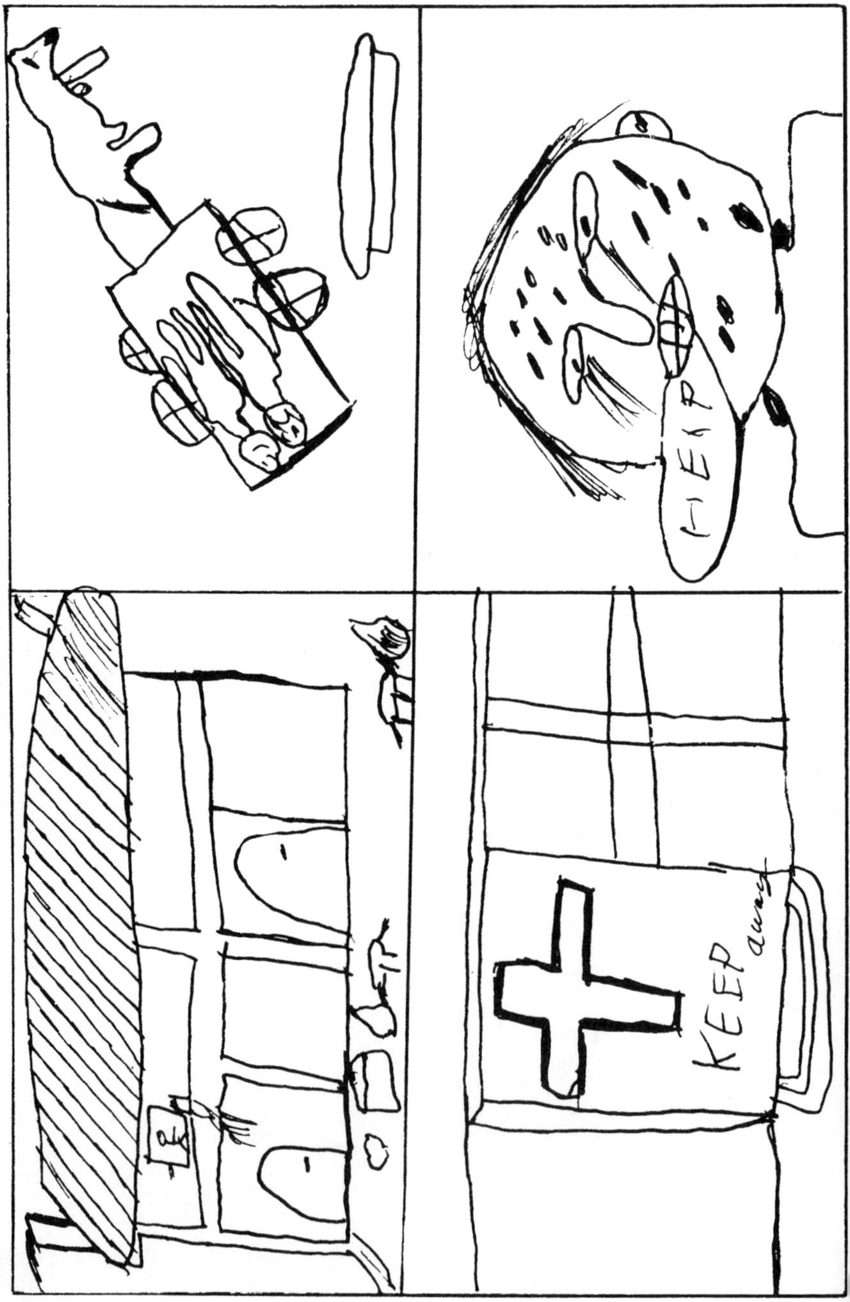

Fig. 5.2   Visual Impressions of the Black Death by Gavin (aged 13)

3 SEQUENCING

As the 'organising principle' of history, sequencing has already been discussed in the context of language and communication (see Chapter 4). The principle can also be applied to visual sequences, such as the picture or comic strip. Indeed, as Dr Unwin points out, the raw material of history is sometimes presented in this form:

> There are many examples of the 'picture strip' technique being used to narrate a story or to project religious or secular themes, including Egyptian wall paintings, friezes in Pompeii, the pictographic annals of the Aztecs, Trajan's column, and the Bayeux Tapestry, of which the last named is probably the most widely used single visual source in school history teaching.[31]

In addition, pictures may be used to explain a story or sequence of events which children of limited reading ability would find extremely difficult to follow in words alone. Dr West, for example, found that primary school children were able to discuss the sequencing of idea pictures in terms of 'earlier and later' or 'before and after'. He also discovered that the study of pictures in history lessons acted as a stimulus to the development of ideas and the use of language, including vocabulary acquisition and the refinement of related concepts[32]. The series of illustrations shown in Fig. 5.3 are based on contemporary prints and depict clearly the sequences in cloth production prior to the Industrial Revolution.

Pictures with captions or dialogue 'bubbles' should serve as a useful transition to coping with more demanding and detailed reading material at some future stage of development. The popularity of comics with less able children has already been mentioned (see Chapter 2, Table 2.3), so the picture strip has the advantage of a format which is familiar and readily acceptable to the children. Indeed, some comics have potential value in the teaching and study of history. In the words of Dr Unwin:

> Some teachers might question the value of introducing war comics – which often glorify violence – into the classroom. Yet children cannot be wholly sheltered from such material, and it is not inappropriate to place war comics in context, to set them alongside other evidence and to discuss them in terms of bias, propaganda, and national stereotypes, as well as considering logistical accuracy.[33]

Visual sequencing through comic strips has been recommended in history teaching and utilised by publishers[34]. One of the most enterprising series of some two decades ago was the 'Classics Illustrated' (published by Strato Publications Ltd), featuring stories by the world's greatest authors in picture strip form. Its purpose was expressly transitional, readers being advised with the words: 'Now that you have read the Classics Illustrated edition, don't miss the added enjoyment of reading the original, obtainable at your school or public library.' However, for the poor reader unable to cope with the demands of the original, I am sure that the 'Classics Illustrated' editions provided rare access to a world of classical literature normally closed to the less able. From

7. The ship carries it to foreign lands.

Fig. 5.3   Sequencing Through Pictures

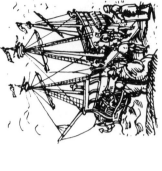

5. Women wash, stretch and bleach the cloth.

6. The tailor makes it into coats and dresses for home use.

3. A woman brings the spun wool to the weaver who makes it into cloth.

4. A shearer cuts off the loose nap so as to make the cloth smooth.

1. English sheep were famous for their wool. Here they are being shorn.

2. Here the women are washing, spinning and winding the wool.

Fig. 5.4 Sequencing Through the Picture Strip

A Roman coin of Hadrian's reign showing Britannia.

IN 78 AD JULIUS AGRICOLA WAS APPOINTED GOVERNOR OF BRITAIN.

Corstopitum
Vindolanda
Chesterholm
Corbridge
Luguvalium
Carlisle

FROM EAST TO WEST HE BUILT A FRONTIER AS FAR AS ROME HAD CONQUERED. IT WAS A ROAD – *THE STANEGATE*. ON IT A SERIES OF FORTS WERE BUILT.

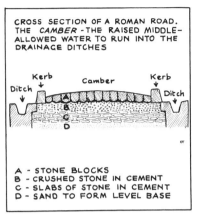

CROSS SECTION OF A ROMAN ROAD. THE *CAMBER* – THE RAISED MIDDLE – ALLOWED WATER TO RUN INTO THE DRAINAGE DITCHES

Kerb   Camber   Kerb
Ditch   Ditch

A – STONE BLOCKS
B – CRUSHED STONE IN CEMENT
C – SLABS OF STONE IN CEMENT
D – SAND TO FORM LEVEL BASE

BUILDING THE ROAD AS STRAIGHT AS POSSIBLE ENABLED TROOPS TO MOVE QUICKLY FROM PLACE TO PLACE.

122 AD – EMPEROR HADRIAN VISITED BRITAIN.

HE STRENGTHENED THE FRONTIER BY HAVING A WALL BUILT ACROSS THE COUNTRY IN FRONT OF THE STANEGATE.

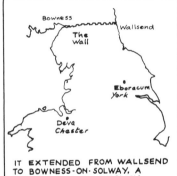

Bowness
Wallsend
The Wall
Eboracum York
Deva Chester

IT EXTENDED FROM WALLSEND TO BOWNESS-ON-SOLWAY, A DISTANCE OF 73 ENGLISH (80 ROMAN) MILES.

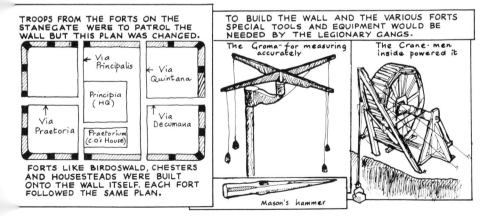

TROOPS FROM THE FORTS ON THE STANEGATE WERE TO PATROL THE WALL BUT THIS PLAN WAS CHANGED.

Via Principalis
Via Quintana
Principia (HQ)
Via Praetoria
Praetorium (C.O's House)
Via Decumana

FORTS LIKE BIRDOSWALD, CHESTERS AND HOUSESTEADS WERE BUILT ONTO THE WALL ITSELF. EACH FORT FOLLOWED THE SAME PLAN.

TO BUILD THE WALL AND THE VARIOUS FORTS SPECIAL TOOLS AND EQUIPMENT WOULD BE NEEDED BY THE LEGIONARY GANGS.

The Groma – for measuring accurately

The Crane-men inside powered it

Mason's hammer

(5.4) *Source*: D. Thornton, *The Picture Story of Hadrian's Wall*, p. 4.

well over a hundred titles in the series there is ample choice for the history teacher.

Visual sequencing through comic strips requires great care to ensure that the presentation is lively and interesting; that the drawings are based on contemporary prints and illustrations to ensure visual accuracy; and that the captions and dialogue 'bubbles' are, whenever possible, based on primary sources, so that the commentaries are authentic.[35] An excellent example of use of the picture strip (outlining the history of the Leeds and Liverpool Canal) is provided by D. Thornton, reporting on materials produced by a History Curriculum Study Group in Leeds. All the drawings and written captions are based on contemporary prints and photographs; and the accompanying based on contemporary prints and photographs; and the accompanying worksheet has questions designed to test pupils' powers of observation, comprehension and sequencing (i.e. arranging statements in the correct order from clues in the picture). David Thornton and his wife have since published their own picture story histories for children. All are based on primary sources and checked by experts for authenticity[36]. An example is shown in Fig. 5.4.

There are many potential uses for the picture strip technique with low achievers in the classroom. Pupils, for example, can be encouraged to produce their own comic strips, using various captioning and timing techniques; they can sequence picture strip frames (presented at random) in the correct order; and they can develop the skills of translation by writing out a story from pictures, or by drawing pictures from a story.

4 PROCESSING INFORMATION

Visual stimuli to the processing of information normally take the form of diagrams. As graphical or symbolic visual aids, they have two main functions. First, when they are presented to pupils, their purpose is to simplify material which would be relatively complex or too abstract if expressed in written language alone. Secondly, as creations of the pupils themselves, they enable the children to process the learning material, and to express it in a form which facilitates both understanding and speed of recall. In the words of Douglas Hamblin:

> Diagrams allow the learner to process information in a way meaningful to him or her. Construction of a diagram means undertaking a cognitive search and selection of elements. Evaluation of their importance is also involved. Strength of relationships can be indicated by the thickness of arrows or the connecting links. Shapes and patterns allow complex material to be apprehended, but more important is the fact that to diagram learning material allows its significance to be retained. At their best, diagrams are more than a cognitive mapping process, for inferences are built in during their construction. Students therefore become more aware of the implications of the subject matter.[37]

Thus, through the use of diagrams, children should be able to distinguish the salient features, classify relationships between components (both unidimensional and reciprocal), and establish groups or categories of related elements.

Diagrams are used extensively in history teaching, but their full potential is not always realised. Some of the most effective uses are listed below, with illustrated examples from recent publications for children:

(a) Diagrams which are constructed to show the relationships between events and between people. Obvious examples are the *family tree* and the *spider diagram* (the body of the spider is the central topic; the legs radiating outwards are the main elements connected with that topic). Another important diagram in this category is the *flow diagram*, which illustrates the sequence of events from causes through to consequences. Fig. 5.5, for example, is a flow diagram, illustrating the interconnected features of Britain's economic success in the nineteeth century in a very simple and concrete way

(b) Mathematical or quasi-mathematical diagrams, which, when drawn to scale, provide visual representations of precise quantities. Statistics by themselves are likely to be abstract to the point of being meaningless to low achievers. The *time line* or *retrograph* is a way of representing the highly abstract concept of time in a concrete visual form; and *pie graphs* and *bar graphs* are similarly useful in depicting such things as population figures and industrial production. A particularly useful and interesting example is provided in Fig. 5.9, which shows individual ration allowances during World War II in very concrete terms

(c) Maps, which, in essence, are diagrams illustrating spatial relationships. These can be greatly simplified to convey highly specific points of understanding. Superfluous details can be a source of distraction and

Fig. 5.5 Why Britain was Wealthy

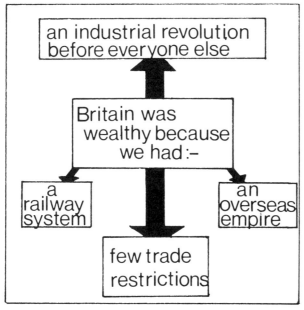

Fig. 5.6   The Population Balance

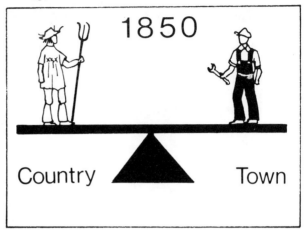

Fig. 5.7   A Lock

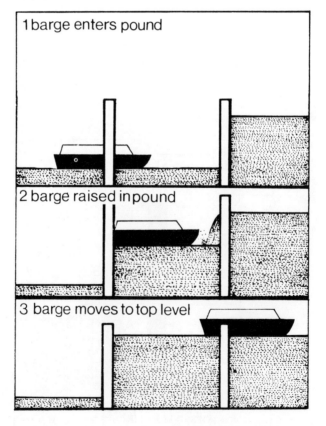

(5.5–7) *Sources*: S. L. Case, *The Industrial Revolution*. Evans, 1975

Fig. 5.8 An Annotated Illustration

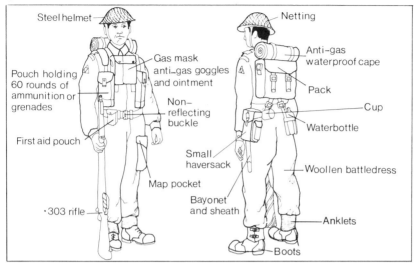

Fig. 5.9 Individual Ration Allowances (World War II)

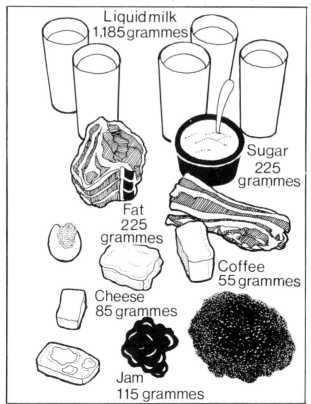

(5.8–9) *Sources*: F. Reynoldson, *The War in Europe*; *The War at Home*. Heinemann, 1980

Fig. 5.10   Two Simplified Maps

should be omitted. Good examples, showing the preparations for the D-Day landings are illustrated in Fig. 5.10

(d) Annotated drawings, which are intended to provide essential factual information. The example in Fig. 5.7 illustrates very clearly and simply how a canal lock works. Another example (Fig. 5.8) shows all the equipment a soldier required for the D-Day landings. From such an illustration, a lively and fruitful discussion can ensue, focussing attention on the need for each of the items. In this way, the children can gain some insight into the nature of the preparation and the problems that the soldiers were expected to face

(e) Symbolic drawings, which are in a sense abstract – even allegorical – but also able to simplify reality and focus meaning and/or understanding on the gist of what is being studied. The visual impact of symbolic drawings (as in the case of emblems) is frequently striking and can, therefore, be an aid to motivation. The concept of population balance between town and country in 1850 is symbolically illustrated in Fig. 5.6 by two archetypal figures standing on scales: the point is made with admirable clarity.

(5.10) *Source*: F. Reynoldson, *The War in Europe*. Heinemann, 1980

ACTIVITY-BASED LEARNING

The enactive mode of representation (learning through 'doing') encompasses a wide range of learning situations. In the context of history teaching, these fall into two main categories: games and simulations. (The latter term can be taken to include both role-play and drama, which are simulated activities.) In practice, of course, specifically designed programmes may incorporate elements of both game and simulation, so that the distinction is not always clear-cut; indeed a series of resources published by Longman some years ago were termed 'simulation games'. However, the distinction is worth making, and each can be examined in turn.

1 GAMES

Although games which are well-designed pay careful attention to subject detail and authenticity (in this case historical), they are in essence liberated from reality. Participants follow the rules of the game – not the realities of history – and usually work towards some goal on a competitive basis. The pupils should be under no misapprehension – the game is make-believe, but it should succeed in providing the children with an opportunity to employ skills and concepts which are fundamental to an understanding of the subject discipline itself. The point can be illustrated by reference to a popular commercial game like 'Monopoly'. Although it is far removed from the real world of business, it should help children to acquire and use skills and concepts which are relevant to business and economics: competition, income and expenditure, profit and loss, buying and selling, mortgages and loans, investment and risk, and so on. Likewise with the history game: although it is pure fantasy in itself, it should encourage children to use historical skills and concepts in a way which is active, rather than passive. There are several types of game designed for use in the classroom:

(a) Board games – Some simple board games, based on such ideas as 'Snakes and Ladders', have been devised to teach children the pitfalls and hazards of certain historical situations, where there is a strong element of chance or risk; for example, the first sailors to cross the Atlantic, or the dangers of working in nineteenth-century coal mines. Several of those published are ideally suited to the needs of younger and less able children, including 'A Voyage across the Ocean in the Middle Ages'[38]; 'Sea Dog or A Tudor Privateer'[39]; and 'The Monastery Game'[40]

(b) Map games – These include location exercises (e.g. deciding on the best location for a cotton mill in the eighteenth century according to given criteria) or developmental exercises, such as deciding on the nature and extent of settlement growth along a valley during the Viking era, or of a town during the Industrial Revolution[41]

(c) Incidental games – Not all history games require intricate preparation; with a little imagination, the teacher can devise elementary games (perhaps lasting no more than a few minutes) to illustrate or reinforce a major theme of the lesson. One very simple game devised by Dr Jon Nichol, for example, involves pupils making envelopes to precise specifications from sheets of paper. First, they make the envelopes individually, taking care to note how long the operation takes; they then repeat the operation, but this time working in small groups, each member having a specialised task (e.g. measuring out, folding or cutting). The point of the exercise is to show that the second method is much quicker, and therefore illustrates the advantages of division of labour – a concept which would otherwise be very abstract. Such a game could be slotted into a lesson on the Industrial Revolution and the rise of the factory system.

2 SIMULATIONS

In contrast to the game, the simulation is a conscious attempt to replicate the circumstances of the real world. In this way, it is intended that the child develops a sense of empathy and awareness of these circumstances through involvement and experience, albeit in a vicarious and simplified form. Various 'detective exercises' (such as those of the Schools Council History 13–16 Project) are intended to simulate the activities of professional historians and archaeologists, and so introduce children to the idea of collecting and using evidence. Other simulations are designed to re-enact the characters and events of the past, so that pupils will develop a deeper sense of feeling and empathy. One method of achieving this is through *role-play*, defined by Morry van Ments as follows:

> A particular type of simulation that focuses attention on the interaction of people with one another. It emphasizes the functions performed by different people under various circumstances. . . . The idea of role-play, in its simplest form, is that of asking someone to imagine that they are either themselves or another person in a particular situation.[42]

Role-play usually takes the form of impromptu drama, including discussion simulations (where decisions must be reached as a result of negotiation between groups representing different historical characters and interests) and debates, where children simulate opposing interest groups in open debate (e.g. MPs debating an enclosure Bill in Parliament).

Drama is very similar to role-play (indeed, when it is improvised it really amounts to the same activity), but, generally speaking, drama implies something more theatrical, involving a greater degree of preparation. For this reason liaison with the drama department should be encouraged, and would be particularly desirable if the play is to be staged before a wider audience; and such a production can be a spur to interest and motivation. Preparation needs to take into account such matters as the sources for a good story (perhaps through class discussion of suitable events, scenarios and historical characters), the writing of a script, the allocation of roles, the making or acquisition of props, and rehearsals. Teachers and pupils may wish to spend time creating their own drama, but there are also some useful plays readily available from publishers[43]. Some of the best plays are what might be termed 'situation dramas', dealing with short, highly specific incidents from the past. This helps to focus a child's attention. Suitable examples would include the trial of Galileo before the Inquisition, or the murder of Thomas A' Becket. Of course, plays need not deal exclusively with famous people. The following example, by Rhoda Power (slightly adapted), is a delightful piece of imaginative reconstruction concerned with the innovation of the printing-press in the later Middle Ages, and how this must have been received by ordinary people. The play is rich in ideas for discussion, particularly how people can be affected in very different ways by new technology. It is also written in simple language specially for the needs of young children[44]:

THE SCRIBE AND THE PRINTING-PRESS

Characters: A Scribe   A Monk   Edward IV
                A Herald   A Crowd of Citizens   The Queen
                Ladies and Gentlemen of the Court

The Scene: A crowd is outside the Sign of the Red Pale in
               Westminster. Inside Edward IV is looking at Caxton's
               printing-press.

Scribe: Look out, you! Stepping on my feet like that.

Monk: Patience! Patience, young man. The crowd pushes me.

Scribe: Patience! I've no patience with a crowd of idlers waiting
            to see the King of England come out of the devil's
            workshop.

Monk: Young man, young man, who are you to use language like
          that! Peace!

Scribe: Who am I? I'm a scribe. That's who I am, and it's Master
            Caxton and that devil's invention inside there that's going
            to throw me out of work.

(*The crowd laughs and mocks him.*)

You'd laugh the wrong side of your mouth if you'd been
inside and seen what I've seen. They pick ready-made
letters out of boxes and arrange them into words and wet
them with ink. Then they put a clean sheet of paper over
them and *thump-thump*, down comes the press and the
words come off on the paper. A page done. *Thump-thump*!
Another and another. And all in a time when I myself
would have been scratching ten lines.

Monk   (*joyfully*): Only think of it!

Scribe: (*angrily*): I hate to think of it! What's the man with the
            quill to do now? Rich men won't want scribes who can't
            work as quickly as printers. I tell you it's the devil's
            invention to take the bread out of the mouth of the scribe.
            And the King of England looking on while it's
            worked!

(*Sound of a trumpet.*)

Herald: Make way for their Royal Graces, the King and the
            Queen.

(*The crowd moves back cheering as the royal party comes out.*)

Edward IV   (*putting up his hand for silence*): Good people, we thank
              you for your greeting. So long as you are happy we are

content. Today we are contented and proud. We have seen Master Caxton's printing-press. We are content because we believe it will make people happy. We are proud because one of our own subjects has brought this new treasure to our country. (*Cheers.*)

Herald: (*blowing a trumpet*): Make way for the Court.

(*The King, Queen and Court move away, followed by a cheering crowd.*)

Scribe: That's right! Go on! Much you care what happens to the likes of me! Faugh, I'm weary of you! Hark! (*Thump-thump from inside.*) At it again! Carpenters putting up a new press! If I could burn it I. . . . . . .

Monk: Gently, gently, young man!

Scribe: (*angrily*): Would you be gentle in my place?

Monk: You forget! I, too, make books.

Scribe: Oh, it's all very well for you. You don't copy for your daily bread. You're a monk! You're kept free of charge, you are! You sit in your cell and copy and paint for . . . for . . .

Monk: For the glory of God and for the spreading of knowledge.

Scribe (*rudely*): Well, I do it to put bread in my mouth. The body has to be fed, hasn't it?

Monk: And so has the soul! And books feed the soul. Hark! (*Thump-thump from the carpenters making the new printing-press inside.*) The printing-press! Do you know what it says? More books! What does that mean? Books in the hands of a greater number of people. Food for more souls. Books for those who never yet had them, because you and I could only copy slowly. (*Thump-thump.*) More books! More schools. (Thump-thump.) More books! More news! Knowledge spreading far and wide. Learning made cheap and so coming to everyone! (*Thump-thump.*) Hark! The printing-press. A hammer forging another link in the chain which binds the world together. (*Thump-thump.*)

Scribe: Ding-dong! A bell ringing my death-knell.

Monk: Not your death-knell, my son. The death-knell of ignorance.

Scribe (*sighing*): Oh well! Perhaps you're right. Come on. Let's go. It's getting late. It's poor comfort to a hungry man when the door of his livelihood's slammed in his face! (*Thump-thump.*) Bang-bang! There it goes.

Monk:	A door slamming on the old dark world and opening on a new one full of light – for which God bless Master Caxton.

(They move away, and for a minute nothing is heard but the thump-thump of the carpenters making the new printing-press.)

The task of completing unfinished dramas is a stimulus to both a child's imagination and skills of extrapolation. Such work is ideal for small group discussion and co-operative effort. Plays may be deliberately incomplete in a number of ways. They may tell only the beginning of a story, so that the task is to write a conclusion or a sequel. They may also be written with blank spaces, so that the children will have to write in the parts for one or more characters. The following is an example adapted from a very old textbook, certainly published prior to the 1944 Education Act[45]. The idea is still a good one. Notice also how the child must read ahead to ensure that the inserted parts are in true context and that *non sequiturs* are avoided:

HENRY VIII AND THE MONASTERIES

Characters:	King Henry VIII Thomas Cromwell Commissioner Another Commissioner Abbot Monk

Scene I

King:	Cromwell, tell me what you have heard about the monasteries.
Cromwell:	. . . .
King:	If these houses are as bad as you say, then there is need for an inquiry.
Cromwell:	. . . .
King:	I accept your suggestion. Special men will be appointed to visit them and to report their findings to Parliament. Is there much treasure stored in them?
Cromwell:	. . . .
King:	Ah, if they be as wealthy as this, they shall hand over their ill-gotten gains to me. See to this matter, Cromwell, without delay.
Cromwell:	. . . .
Scene II	(Whitehall. Cromwell present; enter those appointed to inspect the monasteries).
Cromwell:	Stand forth and give your report.
Commissioner:	. . . .
Cromwell:	And what have you found from your enquiries?

Commissioner:	. . . .
Cromwell:	Have you placed your report in the Black Book?
Commissioner:	. . . .
Cromwell:	And in most of these houses you found evil practices and excesses?
Commissioner:	. . . .
Cromwell:	It is clear, then, that something should be done. (*To the Commissioners.*) What do you say should be done?
Commissioners (*in chorus*):	. . . .
Cromwell:	And if you say they should be expelled from the monasteries, what should be done with all their wealth?
Commissioner:	. . . .
Cromwell:	Let it be so; let their wealth pass into the King's hands.
Scene III	(A Monastery and Soldiers.)
Monk (*to Abbot*):	Good father, what shall we do?
Abbot:	. . . .
Monk:	We are homeless. Our stores are gone. What shall we do? Why is this done?
Abbot:	. . . .
Monk:	Then homeless we must wander.
Abbot:	. . . .
Monk:	Ah, in sorrow we must leave our holy house, from which the cruel King expels us.
Abbot:	. . . .
Monk:	Let us then go, father, to anyone who will help us. It does no good to look upon this hopeless scene.
Abbot:	. . . .

(*EXEUNT.*)

The discussion so far has been largely descriptive. We must now examine closely the advantages claimed in support of activity-based learning. A rationale is to be found in the works of several authors, particularly justifying the use of games and simulations[46]. There are three main lines of argument:

1 Games and simulations are useful aids to learning history as a subject discipline. They are particularly significant, for example, in promoting a sense of empathy. Pamela Mays states the case very well for drama, although her

observations are appropriate to simulations in general:

> Drama involves essentially the projection of oneself into another situation and a
> different role. The actor is, for the time being, someone else. This is peculiarly
> relevant to an imaginative understanding of the past, for in thinking himself into
> the role of a person from another age, the child reconstructs it.[47]

Furthermore, the game or simulation can be devised to develop a wide range of
essential historical skills, such as extrapolation, as well as demonstrating very
clearly that historical situations could have had a multiplicity of outcomes,
subject to such elements as chance. 'It thus acts as a powerful antidote to history
being regarded as an inevitable series of events which has to be learned.'[48] An
appreciation that events could have had different outcomes (the skill of
'prediction') is an essential step towards making informed judgements.

2 Activity-based learning is a powerful stimulus to motivation and understanding. Pupils are encouraged to apply their knowledge and test their skills
and concepts, rather than absorb information in a passive way. Active
participation also fulfils the psychological needs of children; for example,
through social interaction (which fosters positive competition, co-operation
and the skills of communication), an element of play (an effective learning
medium), and an element of fantasy (a stimulus to the imagination). Above all,
such organised activity provides variety in the learning process, and is an aid to
recall through enhanced understanding.[49]

3 Finally – and perhaps most importantly – games and simulations have
been advocated as being particularly beneficial to children of low academic
ability. Low achievers in a mixed-ability class are often put at an initial
disadvantage through lack of prior knowledge, but this is far less likely in the
case of games and simulations which are new to the whole class, so that
'everyone starts on an equal footing.'[50] Active participation is also very
appropriate for the extrovert or hyperactive child who is likely to become bored
and disruptive if subjected to too much reading and writing in an atmosphere of
virtual silence. In the words of David Birt:

> Most pupils seem to prefer this to sitting still and shutting up – but it is again those
> of low ability who are the chief beneficiaries. They may well be in the concrete
> stage of operations, and so 'learning by doing' – as opposed to attempting
> passively to absorb abstractions presented by the teacher – is a vital element in the
> educational process.[51]

For the child who finds reading and writing difficult, games and simulations
provide an alternative means of expression and of gaining a sense of
achievement, particularly through movement and verbal communication.

The efficacy of games and simulations is supported by research evidence,
although this is limited and more corroborative work needs to be done,
especially with regard to children with learning difficulties. S. Hunter, for
example, conducted an evaluation of Rex Walford's *Railway Pioneers*
(Simulation Packs No. 1 by Longman), used with a class of third-year remedial
pupils (aged 13–14) at Cross Green High School in Leeds[52]. The instructions in

the teacher's booklet were followed throughout, and the scheme of work was completed in three stages:

1 An introductory lesson of forty minutes, involving the showing of a film-strip 'which captured the interest and imagination of the class'[53]
2 The game (four lessons, each of forty minutes), which had varied success. There were problems: some of the tasks, particularly those involving financial language (e.g. the keeping of balance sheets and the recording of company decisions) were too difficult, with the result that it was not always easy to to find continuous employment for pupils in teams of more than three. However, certain aspects of the game were extremely successful, particularly the 'chance factors'. In the words of Hunter:

> The drawing of 'chance factors' is the most exciting part of the game for the pupils, and the results of the questionnaire showed that the problems which faced railway builders were well understood. Most pupils seemed able to remember the wording and implications of each 'chance factor' when the game was discussed afterwards. More than anything else, it is these factors which gave the game life, by regularly stimulating the pupils' imagination and reawakening interest at regular occasions[54]

3 The follow-up discussion: 'The intensity of the discussion (and the very fact that there was some) is an indication, in itself, that the game has value.'[55]

The evaluation was based on the analysis of pupil questionnaires (a total of fourteen). This is shown in its entirety in Table 5.1, not only to display the statistical results, but also to demonstrate an evaluative technique that teachers can employ in their own schools. (More will be said about evaluation in Chapter 6.) Many of the questions are tautological, but reqesting the same information in different ways helps the teacher to detect any inconsistencies. From the analysis, it is clear that the children both enjoyed the game and agreed to learning something of value. The main difficulties arose from the more abstract aspects of the game – in particular the financial aspects – and this may well explain the apparent lack of enthusiasm for group work on the part of some pupils. Because some of the tasks were too difficult, some members of the group had insufficient work to keep them usefully occupied all of the time.

Similarly, Rogers and Aston have provided evidence that the enactive mode promotes superior learning in junior children; and there is no reason to assume that this would not also be the case with less able pupils in the secondary school. Two groups of comparable ability (a control group of thirty-five children and an experimental group of forty-eight children) visited an Irish castle as a basis for studying the Nine Years' War and the Plantation of Ulster, both groups spending the same amount of time at the castle. The control group spent its time exclusively on a guided tour and the completion of a questionnaire, whereas the experimental group (although spending some time on these activities) also spent a portion of their visit on four simulation games, designed to facilitate learning through activity. The games – excellent in design and delightful in their simplicity – are fully described by the authors in their article in *Teaching*

Table 5.1   *Hunter's Pupil Questionnaire (In Part Evaluation of the Simulation – 'Railway Pioneers')*

QUESTIONS	YES	NO	DON'T KNOW
1 Did you enjoy playing the Railway Game?	10	4	–
2 Did you find the Game boring?	4	10	–
3 Was the Game too easy?	4	10	–
4 Did you find the Game interesting?	10	4	–
5 Was the Game too difficult?	9	5	–
6 Did the Game go on too long?	5	9	–
7 Would it have been better if you had learned about building railways across America by ordinary means (lessons) instead of by a game?	4	10	–
8 Do you think you have learned anything about railway building by playing the Game?	11	3	–
9 Do you like working in groups or would you rather work on your own?	7	7	–
10 Do you think any of the rules should be changed?	5	4	5
11 If you had the chance, would you like to play other games of this type?	11	3	–

N = 14

History[56]. After a week, both groups of children were assessed: 'Both Test and Re-Test . . . showed a highly significant superiority of performance by the Experimental group.'[57]

Of course, activity-based learning is not without limitations and difficulties. In order that simulations replicate the true historical situation as closely as possible, strict rules of play (often complex) must be laid down; otherwise there is a danger that the children will be side-tracked by discussions and possibilities which are mere flights of fancy and distinctly unhistorical. Unfortunately, many of the games and simulations so far published are very sophisticated and present difficulties for low achievers. The teacher must be highly critical and careful in his/her selection of material. As Evelyn Cowie so correctly points out: 'We are in effect presenting pupils with two complex pieces of learning at once – the game and the history.'[58] Many children from culturally deprived environments might not have learned to play similar games as small children, so what the teacher may assume is a familiar learning experience may in fact be something quite new to the child. In many cases, it will be necessary for teachers to introduce low achievers to new approaches very gently and gradually; it is equally certain that teachers will have to modify and adapt many existing games, simulations and plays to the limited ability of their pupils. Mastery of short scripts and very simple games with few rules will lay the foundations for more ambitious undertakings in due course.

Games and simulations also present difficulties for teachers who are unaccustomed to this way of teaching. There is no doubt that greater involvement and activity by the children increases the pressures of organisation and effective control on the part of the teacher. The teacher must monitor what is happening very carefully to ensure that everyone is on target and that time is not being wasted in a frivolous way. Good planning is essential, but where this is achieved most, if not all, of the problems should be obviated. Time limitations must be strictly imposed, and when 'time is up', the teacher needs to bring the group to a state of quiet – what Peter Slade calls the 'de-climax' – and allow time for questioning and a careful and critical examination of what has been achieved during the lesson. Leading questions to round off a lesson's activities and arrive at a satisfactory conclusion could include: 'What have we learned from the game in today's lesson?' 'What does the game tell us about such and such?' 'From the simulation, can you say how it must have felt to . . . ?' Above all, games and simulations must be regarded as an integral part of a wider programme of instruction – not as something in isolation.

Finally, we can turn our attention to the most recent of innovations in history teaching: the use of the microcomputer. The effective use of the new technology can combine some of the best elements of both the iconic and enactive modes of representation.

COMPUTER-ASSISTED LEARNING

Although the microcomputer is not as yet used extensively in school history teaching (there is a need for more software, and some teachers need convincing that computers are of significant value), it is fair to say that there is no other aspect of historical education which has attracted more interest and attention over the past two or three years. Technological advances have been rapid and impressive. Research papers and projects, conferences and courses for teachers, and programs for use in schools have all burgeoned in a short space of time. There are three main reasons for this.

The first is purely pragmatic: a sense of feeling that the micro-electronic age is now upon us, and that this reality must be taken into account by all subject areas if they are to justify a place in the curriculum of the future. There is, of course, a hidden danger in this line of reasoning: that a subject like history must be forced into some futuristic, Procrustean mould to satisfy the whims of curricular fashion. Other – more convincing – reasons for the use of microcomputers must be put forward.

Secondly, it has been argued – and adequately demonstrated – that computers have value to the teaching and study of history as a subject discipline.[59] Perhaps the most obvious application is in data retrieval programs, such as in the study of local records, including parish registers and census returns. Anne Fay, for example, discusses the use of a data retrieval program with a class of low achievers, looking at ships' passenger lists of the nineteenth century. The experiment proved to be a success, and further work is planned in this area.[60] For ease of handling data, the computer has no rival and in this sense can make a unique contribution to the study of history. Calculations and visual displays can be made in a matter of seconds, so that the children can concentrate on the historical analysis of the patterns which emerge. Another use for the microcomputer is in games and simulations for both simulating the historian's method and re-enacting events from the past. Some of the simulations described earlier in this chapter are now being adapted for use in the computer. And finally, the microcomputer can be used as a word processor and therefore help children with language difficulties to compile a story or historical narrative. *Story Maker* (a new program from Arnold-Wheaton), for example, is an aid for children who experience difficulties in writing a story; and *Readability* (Arnold-Wheaton) is a program designed 'to allow teachers to calculate quickly and accurately the reading age of any text.'

Thirdly, microcomputers are a valuable aid to the motivation and learning of children. The popularity and commercial success of computer games goes without saying. Although teachers have an important role to play, there is no doubt that microcomputers enable children to exercise more control over their own learning and correction. For low achievers, this has particular advantages. In the words of one researcher:

> The Micro gives them a new start with a new method of learning; they are able to accept the correction of the machine without it becoming a personal conflict and strangely enough believe that the machine is always fair to them. They will usually become lost in the relation that they build up with the machine and their concentration span becomes far wider than they would be able to manage in the conventional learning situation.[61]

Several commercially produced programs are now available to the history teacher. Some, like Longman's *Census Analysis* and Heinemann's *Quarry Bank 1851*, are data based. They are undoubtedly valuable but expensive, and financial considerations must be uppermost in the minds of heads of department in schools. Simulation programs include *Drake*[62], which retraces Drake's world voyage, its pitfalls and possible courses of action; and, from Ginn Microcomputer Software, *Expedition to Saqqara* and *Mary Rose*, both of which simulate the activities of professional archaeologists. *Drake* has been reviewed by Adams and Jones[63], who make a number of serious criticisms: the student is not in possession of sufficient information to make informed decisions (consequently much depends on guesswork), and the emphasis throughout is on gaining knowledge of *what* happened, rather than *why* it happened. They conclude that the simulation fails to effect any genuine historical investigation on the part of the student. These obvious pitfalls are avoided in more recent programs, but there is still room for improvement. Taking *Expedition to Saqqara* as an example, I was not impressed by the quality of the visual display and felt that the simulation lacked pace. The activity is time consuming, and would probably work with greater speed and spontaneity if conducted as a more conventional board game. There is also a real danger, particularly with a low-ability class, that frustration will creep in if, after an extended period of play, no discoveries have been made, except sand and more sand. Admittedly, this a problem which faces archaeologists in the real world; but grasping this point through a simulation seems a poor substitute for the reality of work in the field on the lines described by writers like Harry Allen and Andy Reid.

Of course, the quality of software can only improve as programmers learn from experience and bring about refinements. Progress is undoubtedly being helped by major research projects involving LEA's, universities/colleges and schools, such as the Exeter Project (History and Humanities Teaching and Computing), co-ordinated by Dr Jon Nichol of the University of Exeter[64]; and the Joint Schools Council History 13–16 and Computers in the Curriculum Project, co-ordinated by Frances Blow of Trinity and All Saints' College[65]. Already, both projects have produced programs which have been well received in schools; and there is more to come. Of particular interest to teachers of low achievers is the forthcoming program *The American West* (due for publication by Longman between December 1984 and February 1985), which is in part intended for children with reading difficulties and makes extensive use of graphics and symbols, colour and sound.

With the continued development of microcomputers, a prodigious growth in the production of software is to be expected. 'But', to quote Adams and Jones, 'their educational value will depend essentially on a clear definition by the . . . compilers of the educational objectives that they have in mind.' Teachers must resist the temptation of gimmickry and the pursuit of glossy graphics and educational quiz games for their own sake. The teacher must answer the following question honestly: 'Is the microcomputer the most appropriate pedagogic tool for teaching a particular topic to a particular age and ability group?' If it is, then for what reasons? It is also essential not to lose sight of management objectives within the classroom situation. Access to computing facilities could be a problem in most schools, where supply is unable to meet demand, so that individualised learning is unlikely to be a viable proposition, except in specialised computer lessons. Perhaps the best way round this is to encourage the sharing of computers and group work, through which children can make good use of language to discuss possible courses of action. In this way, pupils can develop their social skills and learn from one another.

In conclusion, progress in the field of microcomputers and history teaching must be seen as a co-operative endeavour. I leave the final comment on the subject to Ron Jones:

> To help in this development it should be made clear that teachers do *not* need to become computer programmers. Indeed it can hinder development, because there are so many fascinating problems involved in writing any one program that a teacher can so easily be diverted from seeing the full potential of the micro in the

classroom. I believe that it is now time to organize 'ideation' courses, where teachers can be taught to write detailed specifications based on careful research, and then have this work, for which teachers are already adequately trained, passed to professional computer programmers for encoding. In this way the dearth of good quality software will soon be made good.[67]

CONCLUSION

The Piagetian model has value in that teachers are made aware of the need to make the learning experiences of their pupils familiar and concrete, both in terms of subject content and teaching method. In this respect, the importance of visual stimuli and activity-based learning has been stressed throughout the chapter. Not only do they meet the psychological needs of children, but they are also relevant to the study of history as a subject discipline; for example, in the use of visual evidence, or the promotion of empathy through such activities as drama.

However, it must also be emphasised that these modes of representation are inextricably connected with the use of language, both in terms of 'translation' (e.g. writing based on the stimulus of pictures, or vice versa) and communication, especially through discussion work. Moreover, it would be fallacious to suggest that the visual dimension and activity-based learning are automatically more comprehensible to pupils. The pitfalls of such a glib assumption have been spelled out by writers like Unwin and Pond. Nevertheless, a conscious attempt on the part of the teacher to limit reading and writing to sensible proportions is the first step towards adding variety to lessons and enriching the learning experiences of the pupils. There is convincing evidence from research that the concrete aids to learning discussed in this chapter have contributed significantly to the motivation and historical understanding of pupils with learning difficulties. Free of the pressures and constraints often associated with external examination courses, teachers should be able to enjoy the benefits of flexibility and autonomy in their approach to teaching history to the less able.

REFERENCES

1 J. Bruner, *The process of education*. Harvard, 1960, p. 33
2 J. Bruner, *Towards a theory of instruction*. Harvard, 1966, p. 6
3 R. Thomson, *The psychology of thinking*. Penguin, 1959
4 T. Langman, 'History'. In M. Hinson (ed.), *Encouraging Results*. Macdonald, 1978, p. 229
5 N. Levine, *Language, teaching and learning: History*. Ward Lock, 1981
6 R. Lowe, 'Local history in the school curriculum'. *The Local Historian*, 12, 1976
7 M. Pond, 'School history visits and Piagetian theory'. *Teaching History*, 37, 1983
8 See, for example, J. Fairley, *Activity methods in history*. Longman, 1967; J. Fairley, *Patch history and creativity*. Longman, 1970, pp. 61–63, 117–118; J. Blyth, *History in the primary school*. McGraw-Hill, 1982, pp. 104–112; M. Reeves, *Why history?* Longman, 1980, pp. 61–62

9 P. J. Rogers, *The new history: theory into practice*. Historical Association, 1979, p. 20

10 *Ibid.*, p. 18

11 E. Cowie, *History and the slow-learning child*. Historical Association, 1979, p. 20

12 See, for example, N. Pronay et al, *The use of the film in history teaching*. Historical Association, 1972; T. Gwynne and I. Willis, 'The role of the feature film in the teaching of history'. *Teaching History*, vol. III, no. 11, 1974; C. Hannam, 'A case for the short film. *Teaching History*, vol. IV, no. 16, 1976; J. Duckworth, 'Film and the History Teacher'. *Teaching History*, 19, 1977; T. Gwynne, 'A select list of feature films of use in the teaching of history'. *Teaching History*, 19, 1977

13 H. Johnson, *Teaching history*. Macmillan, 1940, p. 194

14 *Ibid.*, pp. 176–177

15 See, for example, A. Paivio, *Imagery and verbal processes*. New York, 1971

16 C. E. Wilkinson, *Education media and you*, 1971, quoted in H. Eadson, The use of the imagination in the learning and teaching of history. Unpublished M.Ed. dissertation, University of Exeter, 1979, p. 40

17 R. Unwin, *The visual dimension in the study and teaching of history*. Historical Association, 1981, p. 6

18 *Ibid.*, p. 5

19 M. B. Booth, 'A recent research project into children's historical thinking and its implications for history teaching'. *Perspectives*, 4, 1980

20 A. C. Brown, 'Children's questions: a pilot study in history'. *History in School*, 3, 1976–77

21 J. Hull, 'Practical points on teaching history to less able secondary pupils'. *Teaching History*, 28, 1980, p. 19

22 See M. Palmer and G. Batho, *The source method in history teaching*. Historical Association, 1981

23 R. Unwin (series editor), *Openings in history*. Hutchinson, 1981

24 For a comprehensive guide, see J. Fairley, *History teaching through museums*. Longman, 1977

25 H. Allen, 'History trails', in V. McIver (ed.), *Teaching history to slow-learning children in secondary schools*. Belfast, 1982, pp. 125–126

26 A. Reid, 'Archaeology in the cause of mixed ability history'. *Teaching History*, 32, 1982, p. 17

27 M. Reeves, *op. cit.*, pp. 63–64

28 B. Garvey and M. Krug, *Models of history teaching in the secondary school*. Oxford, 1977, pp. 29–30

29 D. G. Watts, *The learning of history*. Routledge & Kegan Paul, 1972, p. 27

30 W. H. Nicholls, A theoretical and practical examination of aspects of Watts' model concerning children's thinking in history. Unpublished M.Ed. dissertation, University of Exeter, 1979, p. 59

31 R. Unwin, *op. cit.*, 1981, p. 41

32 J. West, 'Young children's awareness of the past'. *Trends in Education*, 1, 1978; J. West, 'Primary school children's perception of authenticity and time in historical narrative pictures'. *Teaching History*, 29, 1981

33 R. Unwin, *op. cit.*, p. 45

34 See, for example, the *Flashback* series (Hutchinson); *Action history* (Arnold).

35 D. Birt, 'All ability history'. *Teaching History*, vol. IV, no. 16, 1976, pp. 318–323

36 D. Thornton, 'A history picture strip: the Leeds and Liverpool Canal'. *History in School*, 3, 1976; P. Wenham, 'Leeds and Liverpool: the development of a Schools Council project in one education authority'. *Teaching History*, vol. IV, no. 16, 1976, p. 342. D. and J. Thornton, 1OI Blue Hill Lane, Leeds LS12 4NX, have now published fourteen booklets in their series of Picture Stories.

37 D. Hamblin, *Guidance: 16–19*. Basil Blackwell, 1983, p. 155; see also D. Hamblin,

Teaching study skills. Basil Blackwell, 1982, pp. 46–51
38 P. Mays, *Why teach history?* London, 1974, p. 111; see also K. White-Hunt, 'Simulation: the "Snakes and Ladders" of Destiny – The Anglo-French Struggle for North America'. *History in School*, 3, 1976–77
39 J. Nichol, *Simulation in history teaching.* Historical Association, 1980, pp. 11–13
40 E. Cowie, *op. cit.,* p. 40
41 For a variety of useful examples, see J. Nichol, *op. cit.,* 1980, pp. 14–21
42 M. van Ments, *The effective use of role-play: a handbook for teachers and trainers.* Kogan Page, 1983, pp. 15–16
43 See, for example, K. Nuttall, *Four plays for history.* Longman
44 R. Power, *The kingsway history for juniors: Book 3* (n.d.), pp. 21–25
45 D. Jones, *Pitman's dramatised history: Vol. II* (n.d.), pp. 110–112
46 For a general exposition, see D. Birt and J. Nichol, *Games and simulations in history.* Longman, 1975; J. Taylor and R. Walford, *Simulation in the classroom.* Penguin, 1972; J. Fines and R. Verrier, *The drama of history.* London, 1974
47 P. Mays, *op. cit.,* p. 105
48 D. Birt & J. Nichol, *op. cit.,* p. 6
49 *Ibid.,* pp. 6–7
50 D. Birt, *op. cit.,* 1976, p. 316
51 *Ibid.,* p. 316
52 S. Hunter, 'An evaluation of "Railway Pioneers" – a Simulation game'. *History in School*, 1, 1973, pp. 14–16
53 *Ibid.,* p. 14
54 *Ibid.,* p. 15
55 *Ibid.,* p. 15
56 P. J. Rogers and F. Aston, 'Play, enactive representation and learning'. *Teaching History*, 19, 1977.
57 *Ibid.,* p. 20
58 E. Cowie, *op. cit.,* p. 27
59 For a general discussion, see, for example, J. W. Hunt (ed.), *Computers in secondary school history teaching.* Historical Association, 1979; A. Adams and E. Jones, *Teaching humanities in the microelectronic age.* Open University Press, 1983; F. Blow, 'Teaching the past through the new technology: history teaching and computers'. *History Teaching Review*, vol. 15, no. 2, 1983; R. Ennals, 'History teaching and artificial intelligence'. *Teaching History*, 33, 1982
60 A. Fay, 'The use of the micro-computer in teaching history to slow-learning children: a case study'. In V. McIver (ed.), *op. cit.,* pp. 131–136
61 M. Barton of the Microelectronics Education Development Unit (a Consortium between Bishop Grosseteste College and Lincolnshire County Council), who kindly supplied these via correspondence.
62 A. Payne et al, *Computer software for schools.* Pitman, 1980, pp. 13, 15–16
63 A. Adams and E. Jones, *op. cit.,* pp. 105–106
64 J. Nichol and J. Dean, 'The humanities teaching and computing project'. *Teaching History*, 38, 1984
65 F. Blow, 'History and computers. The joint Schools Council history 13–16 and computers in the curriculum project'. *Teaching History*, 33, 1982, p. 8
66 A. Adams and E. Jones, *op. cit.,* p. 108
67 R. Jones, 'Primary schools: humanities and microelectronics'. *Teaching History.* 33, 1982, p. 8

6

In-school Assessment and Evaluation

INTRODUCTION

There are no universally agreed definitions of the terms 'assessment' and 'evaluation'. In the context of the present study, 'assessment' refers specifically to the assessment of pupils by their teachers. An important element of this takes the form of formal testing, in order to measure learning outcomes and gauge the effectiveness of the teaching programme, but it also includes the more informal assessment of pupil attitudes and motivation. 'Evaluation', on the other hand, is a wider term, used to denote an overall appraisal of the curriculum. The implications are far-reaching. In the light of evaluation studies, teachers will be expected to pass judgements, make important decisions and implement changes when and where necessary. In gathering the essential information on which to make such judgements, pupil assessment is a vital, but by no means the only, criterion.

In recent years, several factors have combined to arouse greater interest in assessment and evaluation, including public pressures for accountability; the development of new curricula and teaching methods; greater emphasis on individualised learning (as opposed to class teaching as a homogeneous whole); and new systems of pupil organisation, particularly mixed-ability grouping. However, as A. V. Kelly points out, in this country, curriculum evaluation 'is the newest and, as a result, the most underdeveloped sector of curriculum theory, so that it is not only the most complex sector but also the most confused.'[1] It is for this reason that many teachers have eschewed the recommendations of evaluation theory. In the words of Professor M. Shipman:

> The contribution of the academic world to the evaluation of everyday, routine schooling has been negligible. Test constructors and statisticians produce techniques and instruments that tend not to fit curricula, and to present them in books that have an opening chapter on the need to assess, and a reminder that concentrates on elementary statistics and descriptions of standardized tests. Curriculum theorists have proliferated but have provided even less guidance. Yet the increased rate of introduction of new developments in secondary schooling has increased the demand for new forms of evaluation. This is only partly the result of anxiety over the impact of new courses and teaching methods. It is more the result

of the need for evaluation to be an integral part of these new, mainly learner-centred developments to secure continuity of learning.[2]

It is for these reasons that the focus of this chapter will be on school-based evaluation. Another reason is that my work is primarily addressed to teachers and student teachers. If teachers have a major part in deciding what to teach and how to teach it, they should also be involved in evaluating how successfully they are achieving their aims. Not only is this desirable as an integral part of the educational process, it is also a professional responsibility if teachers are to retain their educational autonomy.

Our main purpose is a consideration of pupil assessment and curriculum evaluation with specific reference to the teaching of history to children with learning difficulties. However, it is first necessary to examine some of the more general theoretical models of curriculum evaluation. Such an examination serves a dual purpose. First, it provides a framework of analysis, so that certain criteria and techniques of evaluation may be usefully applied – if necessary in modified form. Secondly, it highlights some of the pitfalls and difficulties which are to be tackled or avoided.

EVALUATION MODELS

The theory of curriculum evaluation has long been dominated by the influence of the classical objectives model – the rational curriculum planning associated with American researchers such as Ralph Tyler and Benjamin Bloom, and (in this country, and with specific reference to the teaching of history) with Drs Coltham and Fines (see Chapter 3). The implications for evaluation in this type of model are neatly summarised by Kelly:

> A good deal of both the theory and practice of curriculum evaluation . . . has been set well within the context of an objectives-based curriculum model, and for this reason evaluation has been seen as centrally concerned to help with the framing and subsequent modification of objectives, the assessment of the suitability of the learning experiences to the achievement of the objectives set and the measurement of the degree to which the prestated objectives are being or have been attained.[3]

There is certainly much to recommend this approach to evaluation. It fosters careful, detailed planning and provides precise targets for achievement. The criteria for assessment and evaluation are clearly specified. An extensive list of aims and objectives in the teaching of history to low achievers (based largely on the Coltham and Fines taxonomy) is offered in Chapter 3 (p. 41) – information which is intended to help teachers to plan a structured and balanced educational programme for their pupils. Moreover, precise objectives can facilitate sequential and mastery learning. Evaluation through prespecified objectives is particularly appropriate to the teaching of many basic and mechanical skills, which are of special concern to remedial teachers.

However, as we have seen, the model falls far short of meeting all the requirements of history teaching *per se*. A preoccupation with rigid work programmes and measurable learning outcomes can result in a very inflexible and unimaginative approach to teaching. There is also a danger that lessons will be heavily biased in favour of those elements which can be most easily assessed in objective behavioural terms, including basic linguistic skills (such as reading and vocabulary), elementary numeracy, and the simple recall of factual information. Key areas of historical education, particularly in the creative and affective domains, may suffer by comparison. Furthermore, the claims that objective psychometric tests are valid and reliable are certainly open to question. And, should the teaching programme be deemed a success or a failure on the basis of such test results, the teacher will find little from the testing procedures by way of an explanation for the outcome. The reasons for success or failure must be found through some other means; and to find such reasons is surely of the utmost importance to the whole question of meaningful evaluation.

Weaknesses in the objectives model from the point of view of evaluation have led to alternative approaches. The central concern of the so-called 'New Evaluation' movement is clearly explained by Helen Simons:

> We need to know not so much what pupils can be demonstrated to have learned (the focus of product models) rather what transpires in the process of learning and teaching, the outcomes we could reasonably expect from such transactions and the strengths and weaknesses of educational provision. We need, in other words, to educate our judgements about the adequacy of provision for learning and the quality of experience pupils have.[4]

In this country, one of the leading proponents of the 'new wave' evaluation is Professor Barry MacDonald of the University of East Anglia. As the evaluator of the Humanities Curriculum Project, he developed a more 'holistic' approach to evaluation than would have been possible through the use of prespecified objectives. He defined evaluation in the following terms:

> Evaluation is the process of conceiving, obtaining and communicating information for the guidance and educational decision making with regard to a specified programme.[5]

Thus evaluation was based on observation and an attempt to understand the actual process of education, and had to be sufficiently flexible to allow for a response to unanticipated events. Particularly important was the emphasis on data collection and provision of information in order to facilitate informed decision making within the schools themselves.

Similar work has emerged on the far side of the Atlantic.[6] Stake (1972), for example, sees evaluation in the widest educational sense as a 'portrayal' of 'programme activities'. This he calls 'responsive evaluation' – in contradistinction to the narrower and more limited 'preordinate evaluation', concerned with 'programme intents'. A wider ambit is also advocated by Parlett and Hamilton (1972) in their concept of 'illuminative' evaluation, which is primarily concerned with the description, interpretation and explanation of complex organisational, teaching and learning processes in the context of the 'learning milieu' as well as the 'instructional system'.

There are three essential common denominators in all these 'new wave' approaches to evaluation: an emphasis on education as a process rather than as a measurable product; an ethnographic or anthropological research design, relying heavily on participant observation; and a very wide – almost unlimited ambit – which makes it difficult to draw any meaningful distinction between process evaluation and educational research in general. Although a more holistic approach to evaluation makes up for some of the deficiencies of the objectives-based model, it is itself not free of criticism. Its breadth of scope may render time and resources inadequate; the criteria for evaluation are not so clear-cut; and the results may be regarded as too subjective. In the words of Shipman:

> For the teacher, illumination is not enough. It has to be accepted that many important objectives will never be open to measurement, that some will only be recognized as important as teaching goes on, and that many cannot be identified or defined in advance. But judgements have to be made and those judgements have to be based on some recognizable reference if they are to be convincing.[7]

Teachers should be unashamedly eclectic in their choice of assessment and evaluation techniques, selecting only those which are appropriate to their needs and the needs of their pupils. It is unlikely that either the 'product' or the 'process' model of curriculum evaluation will by itself prove totally satisfactory in the context of the classroom situation, but it can be argued that both models have some value. It is for this reason that S. Steadman, for example, discusses evaluation in the framework of a broad schema, which 'reflects current concerns and blurs the distinction between "objective" and "subjective" techniques – a distinction now outwearing its usefulness.'[8] He therefore considers the techniques of evaluation under five broad headings:

1. Formative feedback on the effects of curriculum change
2 Measurement of attainment
3 Assessment of attitudes and non-cognitive factors
4 Description of the curriculum context and processes
5 Analysis of curriculum materials.

Finally, he considers some of the recurring problems of evaluation: time, sampling, and the validity and reliability of the techniques employed. These headings are extremely helpful in constructing a framework of analysis, and their influence will be evident throughout the course of this chapter. In addition, we must ask a number of basic questions of our approach to both the evaluation of the curriculum and the assessment of our pupils:

1 *Why?* – Is the purpose one of accountability, or is it a matter of providing feedback with a view to implementing changes to the curriculum? In assessing our pupils, are we concerned primarily with the diagnosis of learning difficulties or selection and the allocation of children to appropriate teaching groups?

2 *What?* – In terms of the curriculum, do we take into account curriculum materials, teaching performance and administrative factors, such as the timetable? What are the cognitive and non-cognitive criteria for assessing pupils?

3 *How?* – This raises the whole question of techniques of curriculum evaluation and pupil assessment, their appropriateness and their limitations

4 *When?* – The question of frequency is an essential matter for the optimal allocation of time between testing and teaching, and between planning and execution. Timing also raises the important formative/summative distinction

5 *Who?* – In the context of school-based evaluation and assessment, this brings to the fore the question of roles and responsibilities: of the experienced classroom teacher, the probationary teacher, and the Head of Department, for example.

Having outlined some of the major theoretical issues, we can now turn to a more detailed analysis of pupil assessment and curriculum evaluation with particular reference to history teaching and pupils with learning difficulties. Assessment and evaluation will be discussed each in turn.

THE ASSESSMENT OF PUPILS

The testing and assessment of children with learning difficulties can be fraught with problems. By definition, the less able are likely to achieve only a low level of attainment, so that there is a real danger that tests and other assessment procedures will reinforce any sense of failure. However, many low achievers respond readily to tests when they are pitched at a realistic level because they provide an opportunity to demonstrate success and achievement. There is also a feeling among children of all abilities that courses of study not regarded as worthy of formal testing or assessment are not worthy of serious attention.

The value of pupil assessment will depend to a large extent on its purpose. Macintosh and Hale list six principal aims of assessment: diagnosis, evaluation, guidance, grading, selection and prediction.[9] The first three are learner-centred, primarily concerned with showing pupils where they have gone wrong and where they have succeeded in their studies. They are also intended to help teachers to improve the quality of their instruction, curriculum materials and course design. On the other hand, the other three aims are far more concerned with institutional policies, such as procedures of pupil selection and allocation to ability groups. This distinction between the purposes of assessment is typified by *summative* and *formative* assessment. However, it must be emphasised that the differences between the two are largely a question of intent rather than the forms the actual tests take. There is also a significant degree of overlap, in that particular tests may have both a summative and formative function. The distinction needs to be examined more closely.

1 SUMMATIVE ASSESSMENT

This type of assessment is generally norm-referenced (i.e. a pupil's performance is assessed by way of comparison with the norm established by the peer group). It is also terminal, in the sense that the assessment comes at the end of the course of study. Its most obvious use is in the operation of the external examination system. Within the school, it is commonly used as a means of selecting pupils for appropriate teaching groups according to the principles of streaming or setting. In the case of complete mixed-ability teaching, this purpose will be far less certain – possibly even irrelevant. Summative assessment is also a useful criterion for evaluating the curriculum on the basis of a long-term perspective, say, at the end of an academic year. It is an acid test of meaningful learning, because children will be expected to retain their newly acquired skills, concepts and knowledge over a long period of time. Summative assessment will also allow sufficient time for a curriculum to develop and prove itself: the dividing line between a fading strength and emerging competence is often a fine one, and only long-term observation will reveal which is which.

Summative assessment is most effective when it is based on a system of pre-tests and post-tests. (Criteria for history pre-tests are listed and discussed in Chapter 2.) The value of a pre-test is that it helps to screen out pupils for whom a particular course or lesson is unsuitable; and a comparison of the pre-test and post-test results (when based on identical criteria) helps the teacher to gauge the effectiveness of the course of instruction offered. This is indicated diagrammatically in Fig. 6.1.

Fig. 6.1   A Process Model of Summative Assessment

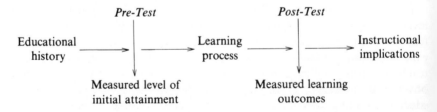

However, summative assessment has only limited value in the education of low achievers, and has potentially harmful effects. In the words of D. Satterly:

> Thus for many pupils and the 20 % or so of our secondary school population who take no formal examinations at age 16+ the prospect of summative assessment seems unlikely to exert the effect on motivation which might be expected among other pupils. Unfortunately the presence of summative assessment can be so influential and pervasive that even less able pupils have come to expect it, with the result that work which is not to be assessed often receives scant attention.[10]

Summative assessment should, therefore, be used with caution. Where tests are administered, they should be well within the grasp of the children and provide the opportunity for success rather than failure. This will depend on the skilful compilation and presentation of the tests. Particularly important will be the establishment of a broad range of criteria, and the avoidance of a narrowly cognitive test, confined almost exclusively to the literary skills of reading and writing. More will be said about this in due course.

2 FORMATIVE ASSESSMENT

This type of assessment is either continuous or carried out at frequent or regular intervals. Its main purpose is to assess current learning by monitoring progress on a regular basis. Feedback is provided to both teachers and pupils, with a view to taking remedial action if performance is unsatisfactory. Formative assessment, therefore, tends to be associated with the following:

(a) *Criterion-referenced tests* – Tests designed to see 'how well a child has done by comparison with some predetermined criterion.'[11] The emphasis is thus on what the child has learned or achieved, and not on how he/she has performed according to the norms of the peer group

(b) *Diagnosis* – The regularity of formative assessment is intended to diagnose learning difficulties and provide a basis for remediation. Many standardised tests in such basic skills as reading have a diagnostic function

(c) *Mastery* – Mastery tests are designed to assess a child's degree of success in learning a unit of work before proceeding to the next unit. Thus they have a diagnostic purpose and presuppose a sequential learning structure. They are a ramification of the objectives model to curriculum planning and evaluation, and some good examples in history teaching are provided by the research team of the New South Wales Department of Education.[12]

Formative assessment has an obvious appeal and relevance to teachers of the less able. The approach is learner-centred and is directed towards providing teachers with the means of identifying the precise areas where pupils are experiencing difficulties. Carefully planned, very prompt intervention by the teacher should, ideally, rectify weaknesses before it is too late, and therefore obviate the prolonged, cumulative experience of failure that has marred the educational progress of so many pupils with learning difficulties.

But formative and criterion-referenced tests are no longer regarded as the panacea. The increased frequency of testing – albeit for diagnostic purposes – reduces the amount of time available for the actual preparation and practice of teaching, and may prove to be counter-productive in terms of pupil interest and motivation. In particular, standardised tests are not as useful as diagnostic tools as had once been hoped, because they are not always reliable prognosticators of aptitude in particular subject disciplines. There is thus a great need to ensure that 'they mesh with the aims of teachers and measure abilities that are worth measuring.'[13] Assessment procedures must be seen in the context of aims and objectives. Another difficulty is that formative tests assess performance only over the short term, unit by unit. Short-term mastery does not guarantee permanence of retention, understanding or future application of knowledge.

Reinforcement and/or remediation through summative assessment and the 'spiral curriculum' are necessary corollaries to formative/diagnostic testing.

Whether assessment is formative or summative, it is first necessary to establish the criteria for assessment, and then to consider the means or techniques available for assessment of those criteria. The criteria should be congruous with the stated aims and objectives, which can be sub-divided into the cognitive and affective domains. These are listed and discussed at length in Chapter 3 (pp.40–44). Cognitive aims, objectives and criteria can be assessed through administering a wide range of tests. Each has strengths and weaknesses, but the range and variety should result in the testing of a similarly wide range of abilities, so that the assessment procedure is likely to be more valid and more reliable. Approaches to cognitive assessment may be subsumed under four headings:

1 OBJECTIVE TESTS

These have a number of advantages including the speed of completion, the ease of marking, their 'objectivity', and their suitability for children of all levels of ability. However, objective tests also have a number of limitations: they offer little scope for reasoning and explanation, they invite guessing, and they are difficult to construct. In a subject like history it is extremely difficult to construct tests which have unequivocal Yes/No or True/False answers, unless the questions are confined to straight forward factual recall. A most useful check list for compiling multiple-choice tests is provided by D. S. Frith and H. G. Macintosh.[14] Objective tests include the following:

(a) *Multiple-choice items* – Pupils select the correct answer to a question from a choice which is offered
(b) *Alternative responses* – Pupils indicate if statements are true or false
(c) *Matching pairs* – the so-called 'heads and tails' exercises of matching names to events, and events to their causes and consequences, etc.
(d) *Sequencing exercises* – the arrangement of statements, sentences, picture strips in correct sequence
(e) *Sentence completion* – the insertion of the correct names/words in gaps
(f) *Word puzzles* – such as crosswords and scrabble-type exercises.

2 STRUCTURED SHORT-ANSWER QUESTIONS

These questions provide pupils with guidance as to the form their answers might take. They help to bridge the gap between the closed limited responses required of objective items and the open free responses sought in the essay question or the individual study. Structured guidance can be offered in a number of ways, including:

(a) Providing appropriate spaces for the answers, and thus offering guidance as to the length of answer required.

(b) Providing lists of maximum marks allocated to each question, so that the children can allocate their time and effort accordingly
(c) Providing factual information (e.g. lists of names, dates, events) or primary source material to act as a framework and a stimulus to writing a coherent historical narrative.

3 OPEN-ENDED ASSIGNMENTS

These generally take the form of the traditional essay or project work. They are of only limited value in the assessment of pupils of low academic ability, because they constitute 'a form of questioning which particularly favours pupils with a facility in language, and can exclude others who have achieved perfectly adequate understanding or mastery of the subject, but cannot indicate this in prose.'[15] With low achievers, creative writing at some length has more value as a means of pupil expression than as a reliable measure of ability. Individual work assignments, such as projects, have value in developing a sense of independence and cultivating various skills of synthesis and reference; but it has already been argued that they tend to be more successful when structured in some way, perhaps through the use of accompanying worksheets which can provide guidance throughout and steer the children away from wholesale copying (see Chapter 4). Open-ended assignments help teachers – albeit subjectively – to assess such personal qualities as tenacity, thoroughness and imaginative flair.

4 ORAL ASSESSMENT

Research evidence, suggesting that the oral responses of low-achieving children are frequently superior to their written answers, has already been discussed (see Chapter 4). It follows, therefore, that oral assessment has the potential advantage of revealing a level of understanding that may otherwise be disguised by a child's inability to communicate effectively through reading and writing. However, oral assessment in history teaching is still very much in its infancy, and is not free of difficulty. It is time-consuming (particularly if conducted on a one-to-one basis), not always reliable (especially in the case of the self-conscious or verbally inarticulate pupil) and requires meticulous care in preparation. Oral assessment may take the following lines:

(a) *Informal–subjective* – This type of assessment is based on the teacher's observation of pupil participation in oral activities, including both group and class work. The teacher is likely to take into account both the frequency and quality of a pupil's contributions. It stands to reason that if such an assessment is to have any validity, then the children must be given every opportunity to practise and develop their verbal skills on the lines discussed in earlier chapters. Pupils must also be aware of what is expected of them
(b) *Formal–objective* – This mode of assessment takes the form of a test. The test may simply be an alternative way of presenting a series of written

questions, the difference being that the questions and answers are delivered verbally instead of in written form. This will be of considerable help to poor readers, and may be assisted through the use of tape-recorders. Formal tests may also take the form of a cross-examination on a piece of work, where it is hoped that interview techniques will reveal far more by delving beneath the shallow surface of a written answer. Of course, formal assessment of any kind runs the risk of causing anxiety for the pupil. This should be avoided by establishing an initial rapport and putting the pupil at ease through first asking questions of a less formal nature. Biased opinions and personality clashes are unfortunate facts of life; and it is for these reasons that two interviewers are likely to be better than one. Between them they can draw up a preparatory list of 'talking points' and ensure flow and momentum in the interview/oral test. Team teaching situations help to facilitate this type of co-operation in the best interests of the pupils.[16]

The discussion so far has concentrated on the assessment of knowledge and skills, but a balanced appraisal of pupil achievement should also take account of attitudes and feelings (the affective domain). The importance of pupils' attitudes in the educational context has been emphasised in Chapter 1. Two meanings, each with different and far-reaching implications, can be ascribed to the term 'attitudes':

1 *Attributes* of personality and character, such as persistence, interest, motivation, enthusiasm and curiosity. Personal qualities such as these are as important as knowledge and skills, but they are more difficult to assess. Macintosh and Hale provide useful guidelines as to how assessment procedures in the affective domain can be made more systematic. They recommend the use of bi-polar five-point Likert scales and the precise definition of terms as ways of achieving greater accuracy and consistency in marking and assessment. The following serves as an example:
  Persistence:
  (i) Most persistent and thorough, will see a task through even if it is rather distasteful. Checks and cross-checks his work without prompting.
  (ii) More than usually persistent – works hard without constant supervision. Can be left to get on with it, is not put off by minor upsets or snags.
  (iii) Not outstanding in any way – gets on with what he is clearly expected or told to do, but does not show undue patience, application or thoroughness.
  (iv) Rather easily put off and distracted. Soon grows tired of a piece of work, needs constant jogging and supervision.
  (v) Very lacking indeed in concentration and persistence. Needs to be watched all the time. Finds it very hard to complete a task.[17]
2 *Opinions* (verbal expressions of attitudes) on the course being offered. Teachers should be interested in what their pupils think about their studies, because such information will help them to evaluate the curriculum. Do the children find their work interesting? Do they attach much importance to it?

Which lessons/activities were the most/least popular with the pupils, and for what reasons? If the teacher is to gain honest replies to such questions it is almost certain that confidentiality will have to be respected; for example, through the anonymous completion of questionnaires. Possible questions, with a view to collecting data for curriculum evaluation, include the following:

(a) What are your feelings about history? Begin your answer

I think history is. . . . .

. . . .

. . . .

(b) My favourite history lesson was. . . . .

The reason for this was. . . . .

. . . .

. . . .

(c) Answer this question by ticking the box which is right for you. Compared with last year, history lessons are now:

much more interesting	
more interesting	
equally interesting or boring	
more boring	
much more boring	

The reason for this is. . . . .

. . . .

. . . .

(d) Some changes I would like to see in my history lessons are:

1 . . . .

2 . . . .

3 . . . .

4 . . . .

5 . . . .

6 . . . .

Of course, pupils' opinions must be treated with caution. Children are rarely the best judges of their educational needs, and what seems like bitter medicine at the time may well be appreciated in future years. But pupils' comments can provide helpful insights and should provoke critical self-examination on the part of the teacher. In some instances, the teacher may feel that some curricular change is desirable in view of what the pupils feel; on other occasions, it may be more appropriate to rectify any misconceptions by justifying and/or explaining a particular approach to the children. This should be part of the educational process. One thing seems certain: pupils appreciate their views being taken into account.

What, then, are the main characteristics of good and effective pupil assessment? First and foremost, assessment should have *validity*; that is to say, it should assess what it is intended to assess. For example, a history test couched in such difficult language that it confuses the pupils is not valid, because it is more an examination of linguistic competence than genuine historical under-standing. Experts define several types of validity[18], of which the most important to the practising teacher is probably *content validity*. In other words, how far is the assessment procedure a fair reflection of the syllabus? Tests should, therefore, be either of sufficient length or sufficient frequency to cover all the essential elements of the syllabus; otherwise too much is left to chance. Question-spotting and selective revision is a fine art at external examination level; but our priority in assessing children with learning difficulties is to establish mastery of the basic skills and understanding of the fundamental concepts and areas of knowledge. Consequently, it is important that all these are assessed, if only for diagnostic purposes. It also follows that tests should be well balanced in their selection of topics; a valid framework for assessment should be based on test items for each of the stated aims and objectives. One way of establishing such a framework is through the construction of a *specification grid*. This entails writing down the aspects of the course which are to be tested in the form of a table or matrix, topics being set alongside specific objectives. The teacher will also decide on the allocation of the marks, according to which objectives are regarded as the most important[19]. Brian Garvey and Mary Krug provide a useful example of such a grid for the teaching of Russian history[20]. This is shown in Fig. 6.2.

A second characteristic of good assessment is *reliability*, defined by R. N. Deale 'as consistency, that is, how far the same test (or a similar one) would give the same results if it could be done again by the same children under the same conditions.'[21] Assuming that the tests are valid, there are two main enemies of reliability: inconsistencies in pupil attitudes (resulting largely from such

Fig. 6.2 A specification Grid for the Teaching of Russian History

OBJECTIVES / TOPICS	Knowledge	Translation	Imagination	Interpretation	Extrapolation	Analysis	Imaginative reconstruction	Formation of logical argument	
Industrialization and rise of Marxism	A 5%		B 5%						10%
1905 Revolution and Reforms				C 5%					5%
1917 Revolutions	A 5%			D 5%	D 5%	D 10%			25%
Civil War							F 5%	F 5%	10%
Collectivization and 5 year plans	A 5%		B 10%						15%
Second World War		E 5%		E 5%	E 5%				15%
Cold War to Detente				D 10%	D 10%				20%
	15%	5%	15%	25%	20%	10%	5%	5%	

Questions A Multiple choice 15%   D Document 40%
B Short answer 15%   E Map   15%
C Matching items 5%   F Essay   10%

(6.2) *Source*: B. Garvey and M. Krug, *Models of History Teaching in the Secondary School*. Oxford, 1977

extraneous factors as mild illness or some family upset) and inconsistencies in marking. Teachers must be sensitive to the first problem by identifying test results which are uncharacteristic, searching for explanations, and not putting too much score by them. Inconsistencies in marking can be corrected to some extent through such procedures as multiple marking (e.g. a whole script is marked by more than one teacher, or sections of a script are marked by different members of the department); listing criteria for certain marks and grades (by way of departmental discussion and agreement); and moderation – to correct unduly severe or generous marking, perhaps through the Head of Department.[22] This calls for team effort. It is particularly important that inexperienced teachers are offered some guidance with regard to the marking of work done by low achievers. If the marks reflect expectations that are unrealistically high, the pupils are likely to be discouraged by their sense of failure.

In addition to validity and reliability, Macintosh and Hale list four further characteristics of good assessment procedure. We have already alluded to some of these, but they are worth listing in full. All tests, they claim, should be:

1 *Practicable* – straight-forward and economical in terms of both time and resources
2 *Comprehensive* – in the sense that the assessment covers the full range of aims and objectives, abilities and skills. This, of course, is vital to ensuring test validity
3 *Dynamic* – assessment procedures should be able to reflect change and be adaptable to differing requirements
4 *Unobtrusive* – assessment procedures should not interfere with normal teaching, and should offer positive reinforcement rather than draw attention to failure. In other words, the emphasis should be on showing what pupils *can* do; not on what they *cannot* do.

A vitally important corollary of pupil assessment is record-keeping. Records provide an overall picture of pupil progress (or lack of it) and the evidence necessary for sound diagnosis and planned intervention by the teacher. This may take the form of a programme of remediation to help the pupil in difficulties; or, if many pupils appear to have problems, modifications to the curriculum may be deemed necessary. Records also provide the basis for reporting – to parents and to pupils. This, of course, raises the all-important question of pupil and parental involvement in, and acceptance of some responsibility for, learning. Such a concern can be nurtured by pupils keeping personal records of their attainment, and being encouraged to comment regularly on their own work – a form of written self-assessment, which helps pupils to reflect on and clarify their own learning. The importance of record-keeping should not be lost in any misconceived progressivism, as M. D. Shipman so aptly points out:

> Unfortunately the vanguard for mixed-ability teaching and individualized methods are often in the van for the abolition of testing and record-keeping as well. In an attempt to avoid labelling and to give all pupils a fair chance of attainment new methods have often been introduced without the additional assessment and recording that could ensure their success.[23]

Perhaps the single most important source of records on pupil progress in a particular subject is the teacher's *mark book*; but mark books are not always as systematic and helpful as would be hoped. In the words of R. N. Deale:

> One of the odder aberrations of our educational system is the view that a mark book is the personal and private property of the individual teacher, which he takes away with him when he leaves the school . . . It seems ludicrous that potentially important information about the children should be lost in this way.[24]

If mark books are at some stage to be used by others, then they must be comprehensible and systematic in their recording. Deale suggests four basic principles in order to achieve this: the separation of marks for different types of assessment, such as classwork, tests, examinations and homework (so that particular weaknesses and discrepancies can be more easily identified); the separation of marks for different types of work (e.g. oral and written work), so that particular strengths and weaknesses can be similarly identified; the clear identification and dating of the work which is assessed; and the clear definition of the criteria for assessment – the criteria should be consistent with the stated aims and objectives.[25]

One of the problems of using assessment and recording procedures which are both highly specific and fully comprehensive is the limitation of time, thus calling into question the practicability of some of the laudable recommendations of educational theory. A way round this problem is to use *observation inventories* and *pupil profiles*, whereby the criteria for assessment are listed, and then ticked, graded or deleted as appropriate for each pupil. In this way, a considerable amount of information can be recorded in a relatively short space of time, although open statements by teachers are not precluded from such profiles. An example is provided in Chapter 2 with regard to the diagnosis of pupil learning difficulties (p. 23). Similar profiles can be devised for recording information on children's attitudes and academic attainment.

An example of this type of profile is provided in Appendix D. This is a European Studies profile, devised at Carr Hill High School, Kirkham, for use with first-year mixed ability groups. Although it is only a pilot scheme, and may be modified in the future, it incorporates many of the features of good assessment and recording procedure:

1 It is fully comprehensive in its coverage of cognitive and non-cognitive criteria for assessment
2 It is formative in that the profile is completed at the end of each of four units of work throughout the year
3 It is diagnostic and aims to establish a minimum of 80 % mastery of each unit test before proceeding to additional work. Failure to attain 80 % results in a re-take, diagnosis and remedial referral, as and when necessary
4 It is summative in that there is an end-of-year-summary
5 It is fully comprehensible and communicative. Both parents and pupils are involved on a regular basis, encouraged to comment and therefore provide valuable feedback to the teaching staff.

The value of the European Studies profile can be ascertained from a sample of comments by parents and pupils:

Melanie: I intend to keep this work up and to try harder in my next core work booklet.

Melanie's parent: I am pleased with Melanie's progress and would appreciate any suggestions in order that I could help her. One thing that she does have difficulty with at school is copying notes from the overhead projector screen.

Linda: I do not understand a lot of my homework. Yes I will try a lot harder in my next unit and take more care over it and I will try a lot harder to speed my work up.

Linda's parent: Very disappointed with these results. I know Linda can do better, but pleased that she has identified the areas for concentration.

Roger: I agree with the comments or compliments given. I will try to work faster and do more work. I will not get into talk or anything else. I find it easier if I sit on my own in class so know one is talk to me or copying.

Roger's parent: Roger needs pushing to do his work correctly and to concentrate much more – if his work continues to be well below average I shall clamp down on his outside activities. I have made him re-do the last two pieces of work. I would appreciate you marking them for me.

Brian: I found some of the work difficult but I will try harder next time but it was interesting and I like doing it.

Brian's parent: We appreciate Brian's difficulties, and we will endeavour to help him all we can. At least he is interested, which says a lot for the presentation of this subject.

Many parents took the opportunity to comment on the system of assessment and reporting. The following statement was fairly typical:

> We are naturally well pleased with Mark's progress so far, and we would wish to add that we especially welcome this type of assessment and the structure of the work to date. In this subject more than others we have a real opportunity to keep in touch which, if we are to support, is all we ask.

THE EVALUATION OF THE HISTORY CURRICULUM

Perhaps the single most important indicator of curricular success or failure is pupil assessment, and it is for this reason that much of this chapter has been concerned with assessment procedures. Results speak for themselves because they help to record progress and attainment in an objective way. There is also value in analysing pupils' opinions on aspects of the curriculum, such as syllabus topics and particular books and materials, especially with a view to pinpointing areas of interest and difficulty. But assessment – no matter how valuable – is limited to locating the problem spots; further information is required actually to diagnose the precise nature of the problems and to discover solutions. This information can be obtained from an analysis of three interrelated aspects of the curriculum: the syllabus, curricular materials, and the process of teaching. Each can be examined in turn:

1 THE SYLLABUS

There are certainly formidable forces for content inertia in syllabuses. Major upheavals upset the conservative members of the department and create increased pressures of work in syllabus redesign and the preparation of new course materials. Radical changes can also be costly in terms of the purchase of new resources and wasteful of old stock which is no longer appropriate to the new course. However, amendments and improvements to the syllabus should be part of a regular and on-going curricular review. Fresh initiatives and developments should be taken into account and reflected in a school's history curriculum – particularly new approaches to teaching and new resources which are appropriate to the school's needs. Issues for departmental discussion could include the following:

(a) *Aims and objectives* – Are they still appropriate? Are they being realised?
(b) *Topics* – Which have been successful/unsuccessful, and for what reasons?
(c) *New publications* – This includes inspection copies of textbooks, which, if purchased, would necessitate alterations to the syllabus, perhaps to accommodate new lines of emphasis, such as the evidence approach, activity methods and modern world history.
(d) *Existing resources* – Their strengths and weaknesses; priorities for requisition within the financial constraints of the department.

Many of the items listed in the Teacher Attitude Questionnaire (see Appendix B) are relevant to discussions about the syllabus.

2 CURRICULUM MATERIALS

Teachers are essentially concerned with assessing the suitability of materials for use by the less able. Although audio-visual aids are important in this respect, it is likely that the emphasis will be on the evaluation of textbooks, worksheets/workcards, and archive packs. Such written materials are almost certain to constitute the bulk of departmental expenditure, and also run the greatest risk of creating obstacles to learning and effective teaching if the language and presentation are inappropriate. A number of useful evaluation checklists and schedules have been designed to help teachers to evaluate such materials through systematic analysis, rather than through relying on superficial impressions.[26]

One such rating chart, designed specifically for the evaluation of textbooks for low achievers, is shown in Fig. 6.3.[27] This is both highly serviceable in its design format and comprehensive in its range of criteria for evaluation. Each criterion is scored on a five-point scale, and an overall assessment of textbook suitability is acquired through calculating an aggregate score of the ten criteria. Aidan Walsh provides a useful list of textbooks commonly used in Northern Ireland, along with their aggregate scores on the basis of this evaluation procedure.[28] Scores above 40 are regarded as good, those between 30 and 40 as average, and any below 30 as poor.

Fig. 6.3   Rating Chart for the Purchase of History Books for the Slow Learner
How to use this chart: Examine the book in the light of the questions listed on the left
hand side of the chart, then give the book a score from 1–5 in the appropriate box. The
meanings of the scores are as follows:

1 Is well below average
2 Below average
3 Average
4 Above average
5 Well above average

Teachers may wish to photocopy this page for repeated use. It would be useful if two or
more colleagues in a school could separately consider each book using the chart and then
discuss their findings.

	CRITERIA	1	2	3	4	5
C O N T E N T	Does the book make interesting reading?					
	Does the book have a good basic story-line?					
	Does the book contain essential historical concepts which are refined to suit slow learners?					
	Does the book cover a substantial area of the syllabus?					
F O R M A T	Is the type large enough, well spaced and uncluttered?					
	Is there variety of presentation?					
O R G A N I S A T I O N	Does each chapter lead to some specific outcome?					
	Does the book have a good index?					
	Is the book durable?					
	Is the book good value for money?					

Title of book: ——————————

Publisher: ——————————

For use with class: ——————————

Source: V. McIver (ed.), *Teaching History to Slow-Learning Children in Secondary
     Schools*. Belfast, 1982, p. 39

In the evaluation of textbooks, teachers would be well advised to pay particular attention to three major areas where they frequently fall short of expectations:

(a) *Language* – vitally important criteria include:
   – presentation/spacing/size of type
   – sentence flow
   – readability/choice of vocabulary
   – adequacy of explanation
   – imaginative stimulus/interesting reading
   – narrative style/story-line.

(b) *Illustrations* – it is important that illustrations
   – have clarity and variety
   – are related to the text
   – have authenticity and are used as evidence.

(c) *Pupil activities and assignments* – these should have sufficient variety to test a wide range of skills and abilities, including:
   – objective items
   – structured short-answer questions
   – open-ended, creative exercises
   – discussion topics for group work
   – games/simulations
   – follow-up exercises, such as suggested visits, 'finding-out' tasks.

The reader may also be reminded that S. Hunter's evaluation of the simulation game, *Railway Pioneers*, demonstrates a technique (based on the analysis of pupil attitudes) that teachers can utilise in their own schools (see Chapter 5, Table 5.1). Pupil perceptions of difficulty and interest (regarding curricular materials) are an important consideration for teaching staff.

3 THE TEACHING PROCESS

Curriculum evaluation must take into account the teaching process. Through observation, it is possible to evaluate how effectively the materials are being used, and how successfully the syllabus is being implemented, in the classroom situation. Interaction analysis theory, which utilises such research techniques as observation schedules, photography and audio-visual recording, is a means of producing objective data for analysis. But one of the major problems associated with this type of research is *reactivity*: the tendency of data collection techniques to distort the reality that they attempt to record. This occurs in consequence of pupils and teachers either 'staging a performance' or being unduly self-conscious and inhibited whilst under observation. It follows, therefore, that any school-based evaluation of the teaching process should be as unobtrusive as possible. It should operate in two ways:

(a) *Teacher self-evaluation* – On the basis of observed pupil behaviour, attitudes and academic progress, teachers need to focus attention on what has gone well and what has proved to be a disappointment. They also need to find reasons and attempt solutions. This is a process of introspection, self-improvement and enhanced professional development, which will take account of principles of classroom management, with regard to standards, consistency, preparedness and flexibility (factors which are discussed at length in Chapter 2); the appropriateness of curriculum materials (on the basis of criteria already discussed); and the suitability of pupil tasks – for example, whether or not they are too difficult, too easy, too dull, or lacking sufficient variety.

(b) *Intra-departmental evaluation* – The monitoring and evaluation of teaching standards cannot rest on teacher self-evaluation alone. As individual teachers, we cannot always be expected to see how or why things have gone wrong. At some time or other, we all need help from colleagues if we are to solve our problems and find a way forward. In this sense, the counsel and support of the departmental team is essential. Group dynamics can do much to modify teachers' attitudes and approaches to pedagogy through such functions as:

(i) *Team-teaching* – By combining teachers who are experienced and inexperienced, or remedial specialists and subject specialists, it is possible to maximise the opportunity for the cross-fertilisation of ideas, and of learning how to teach from observation of the most unobtrusive kind.

(ii) *Direct observation* – Particularly in the case of probationary and inexperienced teachers, Heads of Department will see a need to evaluate the performance of their staff by direct classroom observation; but this will have to be done discreetly and sensitively if the problems of mistrust and reactivity are to be avoided. A stroll alongside classrooms or entry to a classroom on some pretext (perhaps to gain access to the stock-room) are useful ways of gaining insights without being too obtrusive. Scrutinising the work done by children and test results are also important ways of monitoring departmental progress and identifying teachers in need of assistance.

(iii) *Departmental meetings* – These can be held on both a regular and an *ad hoc* basis to consider a wide range of issues, with a view to long-term planning and improvement. Resources, capitation allowances, problem areas, periodic reviews of the syllabus, and the identification of areas of good practice are all worthy items for discussion on the departmental meeting agendas.

The efficacy of the evaluative process will depend to a large extent on the Head of Department, whose key functions should include all of the following:

1 The skilful management of staff with a view to cultivating a team spirit and positive ethos
2 The monitoring of probationers and inexperienced staff
3 The setting of high professional standards and leading by way of example. The Head of Department should show an equal interest in, and concern for,

all the pupils, irrespective of age or ability. The Head of Department who allocates his/her most inexperienced staff to the least able classes is unlikely to command a great deal of respect

4 The provision of leadership in all curricular initiatives, including in-service training, syllabus reviews and the purchase of new materials

5 Acting as the Department's representative in the higher echelons of school management, whose decisions on such matters as the timetable and departmental allowances can have serious implications for the classroom teacher.

CONCLUSION

Assessment and evaluation are an integral part of the educational programme. They help teachers to ascertain to what extent they are achieving success and

Fig. 6.4 The Process of Evaluation

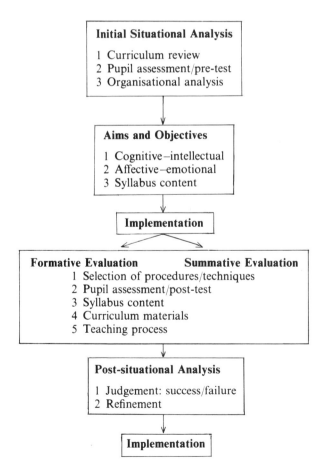

which aspects of their work require modification. Moreover, assessment and evaluation procedures help to make the whole system of educational planning more systematic; they are an essential corollary to the compilation – and subsequent refinement – of aims and objectives. The overall process is illustrated diagrammatically in Fig. 6.4. It is formative and it is summative; above all, it is on-going. From the initial situational analysis, through the subsequent process of evaluation of innovation and change, and then the implementation of refinements in the light of this evaluation, we have, in fact, turned full circle.

Procedures and techniques are many and varied, and it has been suggested that teachers choose those which are most appropriate to their needs. It is unlikely that either a 'product' model or a 'process' model will be entirely satisfactory in itself. Most of the salient features of pupil assessment have been raised in recent months by the new common examination at 16-plus – the so-called General Certificate of Secondary Education (GCSE). Its introduction will have wide ramifications for the teaching and assessment of history in general. First, from discussions with advisers and practising teachers, it seems likely that the new examination will be entered by more than the top sixty per cent of children, for whom the GCE and CSE examinations had been intended. From the grade descriptions already published by the Working Party, it is evident that Grade Six should be well within the grasp of most children who are regarded as below average academic ability, especially if history teachers are to strive to raise academic standards and make the subject more meaningful and accessible to the less able:

Grade 6

Assessment Objective (i): To develop and communicate historical knowledge and understanding
Grade 6 candidates would be able

(a) to recall and display a limited amount of accurate and relevant historical knowledge. Conceptual understanding would be somewhat naive and limited, substantiating examples will often be superficial and/or inaccurate;
(b) to display some knowledge of perspectives of other people but with little or no attempt to explain motives;
(c) to communicate in an understandable form; but the use of historical terminology will be limited and much inaccurate and irrelevant information will be included.

Assessment Objective (ii): To evaluate and interpret evidence
Grade 6 candidates would be able

(a) to show limited ability to comprehend a range of evidence. Candidates' summaries may miss key points, and will give partial and/or generalised answers to questions demanding specific information. The candidate will

find political jargon or language peculiar to a particular age difficult;
(b) to demonstrate the limitations of a particular piece of evidence but only when such limitations are fairly obvious. The candidate will show limited understanding of the need to interpret evidence; will have difficulty in distinguishing between fact and opinion or indicating where a generalisation has little evidence to substantiate it; and though the candidate will be able to list some of the evidence needed to reconstruct a given historical event, the list will be general and show little awareness of the limitations of such evidence or the need to relate it to a particular period or event;
(c) to make simple comparisons between pieces of evidence but when asked to reach conclusions (based on two or more sources) will tend merely to list the major features.[29]

Secondly, as the assessment criteria of the new examination provide a corollary to the most important aims and objectives in teaching history, they are relevant to the teaching of children of all ages and abilities. The objectives are subsumed under two broad aims:

1 To develop and communicate historical knowledge and understanding (e.g. the key concepts of causation, change, continuity, similarity and difference; the exercise of historical imagination/empathy; and the ability to communicate clearly and coherently)
2 To evaluate and interpret evidence (e.g. the skills of comprehension; and detection of gaps, inconsistencies and bias; and the ability to cope with the various types of historical evidence).

A vitally important principle behind the new GCSE is variety of assessment, so that the widest possible range of skills, concepts and abilities can be tested. Therefore, not only will children be expected to write continuous prose but also attempt objective and short-answer questions, 'which would provide an opportunity for candidates of all abilities to demonstrate their ability in many of the assessment objectives'.[30] Many of the finer points of grade-related criteria, the weighting of the criteria for assessment purposes and the precise role of school-based assessment still have to be worked out by the working parties and submitted to the Secretary of State for approval; but significant progress has already been made, including the publication of working party reports and sample examination papers, which exemplify the new approach to assessment. These developments should be followed carefully by history teachers, for they are certain to have major implications for the way we approach the teaching of the subject to all children – including the less able.

Throughout this chapter particular emphasis has been placed on pupil assessment, partly because it is a contentious issue in the teaching of low achievers, and partly because it is perhaps the best yardstick by which to evaluate the success of curricular change. Problems and subsequent refinements should then focus on the syllabus, curiculum materials, and the quality of teaching. As a management issue, it requires a team effort; but qualities of departmental leadership are no less important.

REFERENCES

1   A. V. Kelly, *The curriculum: theory and practice*. Harper & Row, 1977, p. 104
2   M. D. Shipman, *In-school evaluation*. Heinemann, 1979, p. x
3   A. V. Kelly, *op. cit.*, pp. 108–109.
4   H. Simons, 'Process evaluation in schools'. In R. McCormick (ed.), *Calling education to account*. Heinemann, 1982, p. 119
5   Quoted by L. Stenhouse, *An introduction to curriculum research and development*. Heinemann, 1975, p. 112
6   For a useful discussion of this work, see L. Stenhouse, *op.cit.*, chap. 8
7   M. D. Shipman, *op. cit.*, p. 12
8   S. Steadman, 'Evaluation techniques'. In R. McCormick (ed.), *op. cit.*, p. 212
9   H. G. Macintosh and D. E. Hale, *Assessment and the secondary school teacher*, Routledge & Kegan Paul, 1976
10 D. Satterly, *Assessment in schools*. Basil Blackwell, 1981, p. 9
11 D. Rowntree, *Assessing students: how shall we know them?* Harper & Row, 1977, p. 178
12 NSW Dept. of Ed., *Curriculum ideas – catering for the slow learner: history*. Sydney, 1981
13 Peter David, reporting in the *Times Educational Supplement*, 3.2.1984
14 D. S. Frith and H. G. Macintosh, *A teacher's guide to assessment*. Stanley Thornes, 1984, p. 61.
15 *Ibid.*, pp. 78–79
16 For a fuller discussion of oral assessment, see D. S. Frith and H. G. Macintosh, *op. cit.*, pp. 130–133
17 H. G. Macintosh and D. E. Hale, *op. cit.*, pp. 86–90
18 See, for example, R. N. Deale, *Assessment and testing in the secondary school*. Evans/Methuen 1975, pp. 29–33
19 *Ibid.*, pp. 30–33
20 B. Garvey and M. Krug, *Models of history teaching in the secondary school*. Oxford, 1977, p. 175
21 R. N. Deale, *op. cit.*, p. 33
22 For a detailed discussion of marking procedures, see D. S. Frith and H. G. Macintosh, *op. cit.*, pp. 81–97
23 M. D. Shipman, *op. cit.*, p. 36
24 R. N. Deale, *op. cit.*, p. 166
25 *Ibid.*, pp. 166–167
26 See, for example, J. Blyth, *History in primary schools*. McGraw-Hill, 1982, pp. 209–211; C. Hallward, 'Archive units and History kits: an evaluation'. *History in School*, 1, 1973; K. Cooper, *Evaluation, assessment and record-keeping in history, geography and social science*. Collins/ESL, Bristol, 1976
27 A. Walsh, 'Criteria for assessing the usefulness of history textbooks for slowlearning children'. In V. McIver (ed.), *Teaching history to slow-learning children in secondary schools*. Belfast, 1982, p. 39
28 *Ibid.*, p. 41
29 GCE and CSE Boards Joint Council for 16+ National Criteria – Draft National Criteria for History, p. 5
30 *Ibid.*, p. 3

7

General Conclusion

If we are to offer all our children an education that is both balanced and egalitarian, then the principle of a common core curriculum of basic 'essential learnings' must surely be accepted. It has been argued throughout the course of this study that history has a vitally important role to play in such a curriculum, not only in providing a necessary framework and perspective for a broadly based social and political education, but also in promoting skills and concepts that can be both useful and transferable.

Of course, the key question is: how do we make the study of history more accessible to the child with learning difficulties? First, there are some guiding principles of a general kind which can help teachers to obviate the disaffection felt by some pupils in secondary school. David Hargreaves' recent study[1], for example, has expressed concern about the 'destruction of dignity' of so many pupils largely, though not exclusively, through the constant experience of failure. This is prompted by such factors as the cult of individualism (e.g. the emphasis on individual competition rather than group co-operation); the over-emphasis on academic achievement (especially success in external exami-nations) at the expense of personal and social values; and the narrow interpretation of success (seen mainly in terms of intellectual and literary prowess, rather than in terms of practical/manual skills or the expressive arts).

If these are some of the imbalances and injustices that we should take care to avoid, particularly in our dealings with low achievers, then the Rutter Report (1979) provides some positive guidelines to follow.[2] The Report found, for example, that approved pupil behaviour and academic success correlated well with a willingness on the part of teachers to display children's work; recognise achievement through praise (the emphasis being on reinforcement rather than punishment or censure); prepare lessons thoroughly; display trust in pupils by giving them responsibility; and turn up to lessons on time. Such general issues are of cardinal importance to the way history teachers – indeed all teachers – approach their classroom organisation and discipline, in order to promote good working relationships and maximise pupil motivation.

Recommendations should also be related more specifically to the teaching of history to children with learning difficulties. Four issues deserve special emphasis.

1 *The clarification of aims and objectives* – In terms of fundamental skills and concepts (akin to what Bruner refers to as 'basic ideas'), including an

appreciation of evidence and an acquaintance with source materials. The aims of history teaching should be similar for all children, irrespective of age or ability. This, of course, is not to deny the need for vast differences in the complexity and sophistication of subject treatment with children of different ages and abilities. However, even at the most elementary level, children should be engaged in genuine historical enquiry, and not some educational placebo which bears the label 'History' but lacks the real substance of the subject discipline. Accessibility should imply popularisation without vulgarisation. Specific objectives should be carefully planned to take account of individual needs and learning difficulties, so that the learning task is appropriate. This also applies to the planning of a programme of remediation, should the child have encountered undue difficulty or failure with the assignment. It is important that pupils attain a satisfactory level of mastery before proceeding to more advanced undertakings.

2 *New lines of emphasis on teaching method* – The accessibility of an historical education for low achievers will depend to a large degree on teaching techniques which circumvent the barriers of written language. In one way this can be achieved by simplifying the texts that children are expected to read, without necessarily diluting the historical content. It can also be achieved by way of handling evidence in the form of pictures, or research in the form of interviews (perhaps recorded on tape) with elderly residents in the local community. Concepts may also be reinforced through simple games/simulations, microcomputers and communication in small group discussion.

3 *New lines of emphasis on teaching content* – Pupil motivation depends not only on how we teach, but also on what we teach. It makes sense to suggest a syllabus content which relates history to social themes and community studies, perhaps spiralling outwards from family and local history to the national and international communities. Moreover, if history is to make a useful contribution to a child's social and political education, it is desirable that the syllabus covers recent events and ties in with current affairs. Such an argument would certainly find favour with the educational pragmatists who are claiming, with some justification, that schools need to establish closer links with the local community and the world of work beyond school. The rationalisation of curriculum content can also help to eradicate what Sir Keith Joseph recently referred to as 'clutter', which bedevils so many history syllabuses in our schools: the wasteful repetition of themes and the over-emphasis on unrelated factual recall.[3]

4 *The development of resources* – There is a clear need for the publication of more textbooks, study packs, audio-visual aids and computer software to assist teachers in the teaching of history to low achievers. But, above all, teachers need to be directly involved in the production and pooling of their own resources. One way of facilitating this is through programmes of in-service training including workshop sessions, in which teachers can translate principles into practice, pool ideas, share expertise, and co-operate in the production of study kits and other resources that will be of benefit to local schools. The impetus for

such courses should come from the local education authority advisory services and local colleges of education and universities. An excellent example of such a scheme working in practice is the initiative effected by the Department of Education Northern Ireland, which in 1979 and 1980 organised a summer school entitled 'Teaching history to slow-learning children'. Teachers then participated in follow-up group work, and the fruits of their labours were eventually published in the teachers' handbook referred to in earlier chapters.[4] There is enormous potential for initiating similar schemes throughout the country: from my conversations with teachers, advisers and lecturers, it is abundantly clear that there is considerable concern for, and interest in, the teaching of history to low achievers in secondary schools.

Continued progress in the field of teaching history to children with learning difficulties calls for an inter-disciplinary approach to both educational research and teacher training and professional development. Key areas for investigation include the aims and objectives of history teaching and child psychology – both behavioural (particularly regarding pupil attitudes and motivation) and developmental (regarding stages of cognitive and emotional growth and readiness for learning). We also need to be concerned with areas of curriculum theory and development (not only regarding history *per se* but also its place in the context of the whole curriculum), aspects of school and pupil organisation (particularly mixed-ability grouping, etc.), assessment and evaluation. Above all, there is a need to disseminate the principles of remedial/compensatory education on a much wider basis – no less than an infusion of fundamental teaching skills for the less able across the whole curriculum. This assertion has far-reaching implications for the content of basic teacher training, as well as some of the priorities that are given to the continuing education and professional development of serving teachers.

REFERENCES

1 D. Hargreaves, *The challenge for the comprehensive school.* Routledge & Kegan Paul, 1982
2 M. Rutter et al, *Fifteen thousand hours.* Open Books, 1979, pp. 182–98
3 K. Joseph, 'Why teach history in school?' *The Historian*, no. 2, 1984
4 V. McIver (ed.), *Teaching history to slow-learning children in secondary schools.* Belfast, 1982

Appendix A

PUPIL ATTITUDE QUESTIONNAIRE (PAQ)

Name and Form . . . .

School . . . .

Age . . . . years . . . . months

Date of birth . . . .

Below you will find some questions about schoolwork. Answer the questions by putting a tick (✓) in the box by the answer which is right for you. There are no right or wrong answers and no trick questions. This is not a test, and no-one will be told your answers. But you must tell the TRUTH and you must answer ALL the questions. If you get stuck, please raise your hand and ask for help.

SECTION 1

Here are some questions to find out what you think of school. Put a tick in the box by the answer which is right for you.

1 Are you happy at school?

       nearly all the time

       much of the time

       about half the time

       sometimes

       rarely or never

2 How soon would you like to leave school or college and start work?

       as soon as possible

       when you are 16

       when you are 17

       when you are 18

       when you are over 18

3 Do you work hard at school?

        nearly all the time

        much of the time

        about half the time

        sometimes

        rarely or never

4 In general, would you say you do well in your school work?

        nearly all the time

        much of the time

        about half the time

        sometimes

        rarely or never

5 In general, is your behaviour towards your teachers:

        very helpful

        quite helpful

        indifferent (neither helpful or unhelpful)

        often unhelpful

        very unhelpful

6 In class, does your mind wander off what you should be doing?

        most of the time

        quite a lot

        occasionally

        rarely

        very rarely or never

7 Do you think school is a waste of time?

        nearly all the time

        much of the time

        about half the time

        sometimes

        rarely or never

8 Do you find school dull or boring?

     nearly all the time

     much of the time

     about half the time

     sometimes

     rarely or never

9 In general, what are your feelings towards tests?

     strongly like

     like

     undecided

     dislike

     strongly dislike

10 How important is your wish to do better at school?

     very important

     fairly important

     undecided

     fairly unimportant

     very unimportant

SECTION 2

Here are some questions to find out what you think of HISTORY. They are very similar to the questions you have just answered. Put a tick in the box by the answer which is right for you.

1 Do you enjoy your history lessons?

     nearly all the time

     much of the time

     about half the time

     sometimes

     rarely or never

2 How soon would you like to stop learning history?

    as soon as possible

    when you are 16

    when you are 17

    when you are 18

    when you are over 18

3 Do you work hard in your history lessons?

    nearly all the time

    much of the time

    about half the time

    sometimes

    rarely or never

4 Would you say you do well in history?

    nearly all the time

    much of the time

    about half the time

    sometimes

    rarely or never

5 Is your behaviour towards your history teacher:

    very helpful

    quite helpful

    indifferent (neither helpful nor unhelpful)

    often unhelpful

    very unhelpful

6 In history lessons does your mind wander off what you should be doing?

    most of the time

    quite a lot

    occasionally

    rarely

    very rarely or never

7 Do you think history lessons are a waste of time?

     nearly all the time

     much of the time

     about half the time

     sometimes

     rarely or never

8 Do you find history dull or boring?

     nearly all the time

     much of the time

     about half the time

     sometimes

     rarely or never

9 What do you feel about history tests?

     strongly like

     like

     undecided

     dislike

     strongly dislike

10 How important is your wish to do better in history?

     very important

     fairly important

     undecided

     fairly unimportant

     very unimportant

SECTION 3

Below are some statements about HISTORY. Please indicate how strongly you agree or disagree with each statement by ticking the box which is right for you.

STATEMENTS	Strongly Agree	Agree	Undecided	Disagree	Strongly Disagree
History lessons make school more interesting					
Many good stories are taken from history					
It is a good pastime to read history books from the library					
There are some exciting films and TV programmes on history					
Places like museums are well worth a visit					
Knowing about the past (History) helps us to understand the present					
It is important to work hard in history to get qualifications					
It is important to work hard in history to get good marks					
Getting bad marks in history upsets me					
I work hard in history lessons to please the teacher					

SECTION 4

Below is a list of school subjects. Please indicate how interesting or boring you find each one by ticking the boxes which are right for you.

SUBJECT	Very Interesting	Interesting	Undecided	Boring	Very Boring
English					
Maths					
Science					
History					
Geography					
RE					
PE/Games					
Art					
Music					
Craft					

Below is the same list again. This time please indicate how important you think each subject is by ticking the boxes which are right for you.

SUBJECT	Very Important	Important	Undecided	Un-important	Very Un-important
English					
Maths					
Science					
History					
Geography					
RE					
PE/Games					
Art					
Music					
Craft					

SECTION 5

Please answer the questions below by writing short answers in the spaces provided.

1 What is history?   Begin your answer

History is . . . .
. . . .
. . . .

2 What are your feelings about history?   Begin your answer

I think history is . . . .
. . . .
. . . .

3 What changes would you like to make to your history lessons? Begin your answer:

Some of the changes I would like to make to history lessons are:

1 . . . .

2 . . . .

3 . . . .

4 . . . .

5 . . . .

6 . . . .

SECTION 6

Please answer the questions by ticking the box which is right for you. Give reasons for your choice of answer in the space provided.

1 Compared with last year, my schoolwork is now:

much more interesting

more interesting

equally interesting or boring

more boring

much more boring

The reason for this is . . . .
. . . .
. . . .

2 Compared with last year, history lessons are now:

much more interesting

more interesting

equally interesting or boring

more boring

much more boring

The reason for this is . . . .

. . . .

. . . .

SECTION 7

Below is a list of questions about your interests and pastimes. Most will require only YES or NO answer, but some will need a sentence. Answer each question in the space provided.

1 Which school subject do you like best? . . . .

Why?. . . . .

. . . .

2 Do you do any painting or drawing out of school hours?

. . . .

3 Do you make anything?. . . . .

4 What do you like doing best at home?. . . . .

. . . .

5 What would you like to do when you leave school? . . . .

. . . .

Why?. . . . .

. . . .

6 Do you collect anything? . . . .

What is it? . . . .

7 Do you like reading? . . . .

8 What do you read in your spare time?. . . . .

. . . .

9 Write down the names of any books, papers or magazines which you have read
recently . . . .

. . . .

. . . .

10 Do you ever go for short journeys from home? . . . .

What do you visit? . . . .

. . . .

Why? . . . .

. . . .

11 Which country would you like to visit most? . . . .

12 Do you belong to any club or organisation?. . . . .

13 How many nights do you go out during the week?. . . . .

14 When you go out, what do you like to do? . . . .

. . . .

Why? . . . .

. . . .

Appendix B

TEACHER ATTITUDE QUESTIONNAIRE (TAQ)

Name . . . .

School . . . .

Status . . . .

Number of Years Teaching . . . .

The following questions relate to the teaching of history to slow learners in their third year at secondary school (Age: 13–14). Slow learners may be defined for this purpose as 'pupils of below-average ability'.
All replies will be treated as strictly confidential

1 Does your history syllabus have stated aims or objectives?
 Please delete as appropriate   YES/NO

2 If your answer was YES, how successful/unsuccessful do you think your syllabus aims/objectives are in practice? Please indicate by ticking the appropriate point on the following rating scale:

 Successful:——:——:——:——:——:——:——: Unsuccessful

3 How important would you say history is in your school in meeting the educational needs of slow learners? Please tick

 Important:——:——:——:——:——:——: Unimportant

4 Does history become an optional subject for slow learners at any stage between first and fifth year?
 Please delete   YES/NO

5 If your answer was YES, please indicate when the subject becomes optional

. . . .

6 Please list TWO topics which have achieved more success than expected:

 1 . . . .

 2 . . . .

 Briefly comment on the reasons for their success: . . . .

 . . . .

 . . . .

 . . . .

7 Please list TWO topics which have been a disappointment:

1 . . . .

2 . . . .

Briefly comment on the reasons for their failure: . . . .

. . . .

. . . .

. . . .

8 Please indicate your weekly time allocation/number of lessons for third-year remedial history. . . . .

9 In teaching history to the third year slow learners, which timetable would you prefer? Please tick appropriate box.

A single periods (30–45 mins)

B double periods (60–90 mins)

C a combination of A and B

D block time (over 90 mins)

E other (please specify)

Briefly comment on the reasons for your choice . . . .

. . . .

. . . .

. . . .

10 With reference to question 9, are you provided with a timetable of your choice?
YES/NO

11 On the basis of existing practice in your school, please indicate the degree of importance of liaison between the History and Remedial departments. Tick the appropriate point on the rating scale:

Important:——:——:——:——:——:——::——:Unimportant

12 If such liaison takes place, please list the reasons

1 . . . .

2 . . . .

3 . . . .

4 . . . .

5 . . . .

13 Please indicate the degree of importance attached to formal tests in teaching history to slow learners. (Please tick)

Important:——:——:——:——:——:——:—: Unimportant

14 On the basis of existing practice, what importance does your History department attach to the display of work done by slow learners? (Please tick)

Important:——:——:——:——:——:——:—Unimportant

15 Please indicate the titles of TWO textbooks most often used with your slow learners. For each there is a list of five criteria by which the overall suitability of the textbooks can be assessed. Please tick each of the five according to the rating scale.

TEXTBOOK	Excellent	Good	Fair	Poor	Very Poor
Title:					
a Pictures					
b Maps					
c Diagrams					
d Facts					
e Language					
Title:					
a Pictures					
b Maps					
c Diagrams					
d Facts					
e Language					

16 Please list FOUR most important pupil activities in your History lessons. List them in order of importance commencing with the most important:

1 . . . .

2 . . . .

3 . . . .

4 . . . .

17 Below is a list of possible problems in teaching history to slow learners. Please indicate the degree of importance you attribute to each problem in your own school by ticking the rating scale, ranging from Important (serious problem) to Unimportant (no problem).

		Important	Unimportant
1	Disruptive behaviour	——:——:——:——:——:——:——
2	Absenteeism	——:——:——:——:——:——:——
3	Limited pupil concentration	——:——:——:——:——:——:——
4	Lack of pupil motivation	——:——:——:——:——:——:——
5	Syllabus content	——:——:——:——:——:——:——
6	Range of pupil ability	——:——:——:——:——:——:——
7	Textbook suitability	——:——:——:——:——:——:——
8	History is compulsory	——:——:——:——:——:——:——
9	Pupil immaturity	——:——:——:——:——:——:——
10	Unsupportive Remedial Dept.	——:——:——:——:——:——:——
11	Unsupportive parents	——:——:——:——:——:——:——
12	Timetable arrangements	——:——:——:——:——:——:——
13	Lack of specialised training	——:——:——:——:——:——:——

If there are many other difficulties please specify below:

1 . . . .

2 . . . .

3 . . . .

4 . . . .

Appendix C

TWO SAMPLE WORKSHEETS BASED ON PRIMARY SOURCES

1 This picture was taken in about 1890. How many years ago was that?

2 Copy this sentence and fill in the missing words:
   The picture shows a s . . . . on a s . . . . c . . . .

3 Find the name of the owner of the shop. Which street was it on? What kind of shop was it?

4 How many people are in the picture? Did the photographer take them by surprise?

5 Imagine you have gone back in time. You meet the men in the picture. Think of THREE questions to ask them. Write them down.

6 Write about anything in the picture. It should be interesting.

A DIARY NEARLY ONE HUNDRED YEARS OLD

TALKING POINT

Have you ever kept a DIARY? Do you keep a diary now? Write down some reasons why people keep diaries. What sort of things do you put in your diary? Start right away. We will stop in about five minutes.

MR WILLIAM DENNIS

Just imagine for a moment that it is the year 2081 – a hundred years into the future. If someone found your diary, they would certainly find it interesting. Your diary would by then be part of HISTORY. William Dennis was a farmer's son from Sutton Bridge in Lincolnshire. You can see an old photograph above of William with his wife Kate. William kept a diary for six years. He started in 1883 when he was nineteen. The diary has 185 pages full of interesting details about life as it was nearly 100 years ago.

These are some of the ENTRIES in the diary. A few strange words have been slightly changed or left out, but this has not changed the meaning of anything William said.

October 24th, 1883: Saw Tom Naylor sell some wheat for 28s (£1.40) a quarter at Peterborough Market. The trade is very bad, but we keep hoping for better things. Mr. John Bright, MP for Birmingham, made a fine speech at Leeds a week ago. He said that more people should be allowed to VOTE. He mentioned other REFORMS, such as the ending of slavery, and said that the LIBERALS had done it. He said the TORIES were against all that was good.

December 14th, 1883: This was Long Sutton Fat Stock Show. Most of it made a fair price, about 10s (50p) a stone for beef and 9d (nearly 4p) a pound for mutton. Pork is very cheap.

April 3rd, 1884: Mr Gladstone made one of the most cutting speeches ever known in the HOUSE OF COMMONS, dressing down the Tories.

September 13th, 1884: Kate Chatterton (girlfriend) gave me the 'sack' – the only reason she gave was that she did not love me.

October 20th, 1884: I went to London – had Fred Burgess for a mate. We left Sutton Bridge at 5.40 a.m. and reached King's Cross at 9.30 a.m. We took a train to South Kensington and went straight to the Health Exhibition. This was an exhibition of everything to do with the body, such as food, dress and household things. We were walking about from one o'clock till seven. The gardens were beautifully lit up with an electric light, and to see the fountains was something grand.

November 28th, 1885: I went to Birmingham to visit the Cattle Show. But my main reason was to see my old sweetheart (Kate Chatterton). We walked to the arcade and bought a ring for Kate. We explained ourselves and renewed the engagement. We were determined to help each other all we could both as regards this world and that which is to come.

February, 1886: There has been a riot in London. There are so many UNEMPLOYED that the other day thousands met in Trafalgar Square, and then went on to break windows and take things from shops to the value of thousands of pounds.

QUESTIONS

1 Copy down this list of 'HEADS' into your book. Put each on a separate line:

  (a) *Reforms*
  (b) *Vote*
  (c) *Liberals*

   (d) *Tories*
   (e) *House of Commons*
   (f) *Unemployed people*

2 Now copy out the 'TAILS' alongside the 'HEADS'. Be sure to match them properly:
   – *people without jobs*
   – *a political party now led by Mr David Steel*
   – *a place in Parliament where MPs change old laws or make new laws for people*
   – *changes or improvements in the laws*
   – *a political party now usually called the Conservative party*
   – *to be able to take part in an election (choosing) of Members of Parliament*

3 In which year did Mr William Dennis start his diary? How many years ago was that?

4 Copy the table of the things which interested Mr Dennis. In the first column is the list of interests. In the second column is a list of diary dates when each interest is mentioned. In the third column some details are given from the diary. Complete the table. The first line has been done to help you.

INTERESTS	DATE OF ENTRY	DETAILS OF THE ENTRY
Politics	Oct. 24, 1883	Mentions the speech of Mr. Bright, MP (Liberal)
Farming		
Romance		
Visits		

5 Look at the photograph of William Dennis and his wife Kate and read the entries for September 13th 1884 and November 28th 1885. What can you say about the romance between them?
6 Look carefully at the picture on the International Health Exhibition 1884. (This picture is not supplied here.)
   (a) *Draw a picture of a lady and gentleman of 1884.*
   (b) *List THREE differences between the clothes they wore and the way people dress today.*
7 Choose an interesting day in your life. Write a page in your diary for that day. Put down the things which you think will most interest a boy or a girl living 100 years from now in the year 2081. This list should help you:
FRIENDS, FAMILY, INTERESTING VISITS, TRAVEL, ROMANCE,

PRICES, LOCAL NEWS, WORLD NEWS, JOB SITUATION, SCHOOL
8 Write about anything in William Dennis' diary which you find very interesting. Draw some pictures if you wish. Perhaps you would like to know what I find interesting:
(a) *Prices for various things – how different they are today.*
(b) *What Mr Dennis thought about politics – which Party he must have supported.*
(c) *How long a train journey took compared with today.*
(d) *Problems in the streets of London – riots then compared with riots in recent months.*

Appendix D
European Studies Profile

TEACHER'S GUIDE TO THE EUROPEAN STUDIES PROFILE

This profile aims to give the maximum information about the pupils studying this subject, to as many people as possible, using as little time as possible.

INFORMATION

Any relevant information concerning a pupil not covered in the set categories can be given in the space allocated for other comments at the end of each unit.

PEOPLE TO WHOM THE PROFILE WILL BE AVAILABLE

All teaching staff. The pupil concerned. Parents of pupil concerned. Any other person to whom the headmaster has given permission to see it.

TIME

As far as possible one double period at the end of each unit will be set aside for staff to complete the profiles. i.e. I intend to usefully occupy the pupils (e.g. in a lead lesson) and so allow staff free time to do this work.

COMPLETION OF PROFILES

There are four units in the school year. A profile will be completed for each of these units. Each profile will be identical in format but the section 'Skills acquired' will differ in each unit.
NB Staff are free to underline *as many statements* as they wish in each category.

The section of 'Handwriting and Presentation of Work' will be discussed at a department meeting. This is to enable us to agree on common standards.

Pupils *must* be encouraged to complete their section on the profile. They may need some guide lines at first until they are familiar with the idea of self assessment. Whilst pupils are usually willing to write down their bad points they are often reluctant to admit to their achievements in case they are mistaken as being 'Big-Headed'. At some stage they will have to learn how to present themselves in a favourable light (e.g. Application forms) therefore they should be encouraged to recognise their achievements as well as failures.

Whilst a profile must be honest if it is to be of any value, it should *as far as possible* have a positive attitude stressing achievement rather than failure.

As the pupil has the opportunity to write his/her own comments it is possible they may disagree with one of your statements. This means the statements must be read thoroughly and underlined with care i.e. You must be able to support your decisions.

IMPORTANT

This is only a pilot scheme. Your comments *including criticism* will be of great value to myself as well as to others intending to try a similar scheme. If you wish to discuss your feelings about this profile with other members of staff, be they good or bad, please do, but please tell me as well. Only by doing this will we be able to devise a profile which is acceptable to most members of the European Studies Team.

NAME:———————————————   FORM————————————————

EUROPEAN STUDIES

Whilst the categories below do not cover every eventuality it is hoped that this profile will give you a good guide of the progress made by the above pupil in *this subject*.

Core Work and Additional Work Grades are based on the following marks.

GRADE A 45–50   GRADE B 35–44
GRADE C 25–34   GRADE D 15–24
GRADE E Below 14

The Effort Grades are based on the teacher's view of the effort made by the pupil in relation to classwork, homework and behaviour.

A = Excellent   B = Good   C = Satisfactory
D = Little Effort Made   E = Poor

UNIT A

CONTENT

The World and Europe. Europe in Outline. Europe and World War Two. Europe rises from the ashes and the EEC.

CORE WORK

/50 GRADE A B C D E

EFFORT

GRADE A B C D E

TEST

/50 GRADE A B C D E   (First Attempt)

Pupils who do not gain at least 40/50 for the test at their first attempt must re-take it until they gain this mark. Only then are they allowed to start additional work.

ADDITIONAL WORK

/50   GRADE   A   B   C   D   E

EFFORT

GRADE   A   B   C   D   E

HANDWRITING AND PRESENTATION OF WORK

Excellent. Good. Satisfactory. Sometimes untidy. Often untidy. Poor. Sometimes illegible. Difficult to read.

SPELLING

Seldom makes mistakes even with complex words.
Can cope with basic words but has some difficulty with new terminology.
Competent with everyday spelling.
Can cope with most basics.
Has difficulty with very basic words.

ATTITUDE TO WORK

Inquisitive.	Does only what is required.
Lazy.	Interested.
Enthusiastic.	Does more than required.
Appears uninterested.	Moderately interested.
Reluctant to do written work	Good keen pupil.
Usually undeterred by	Conscientious in approach to problems.
difficulties.	Takes a pride in work.
Lacks persistence.	Prepared to listen to advice.
Can be lazy.	

OVERALL ABILITY

Has ability with very basic work but finds comprehension and written work difficult.
Has ability and produces work of a good standard.
Has ability but tries to work too quickly making too many mistakes.
Has ability with core work but finds additional work difficult.
Has shown ability but does not always use it.
Has a very high ability working quickly and accurately.
Has ability but needs to work with more speed and cover more work.

ABILITY TO WORK INDEPENDENTLY

Able to work on own when required.
Able to work on own with a little guidance.
Able to work on own with a lot of guidance.
Continual guidance needed.

HOMEWORK

Always completed to a satisfactory standard.
Usually completed to a satisfactory standard.
Seldom completed to a satisfactory standard.
Never completed to a satisfactory standard.
Always handed in at time appointed.

Usually handed in at time appointed.
Seldom handed in at time appointed.
Never handed in at time appointed.

SKILLS ACQUIRED IN CORE WORK (C) AND ADDITIONAL WORK (A)

C
Able to locate the six continents on a map.
Able to locate the main oceans on a map.
Able to use the Index and Table of Contents in an Atlas.
Able to locate the information required on political and physical maps.
Able to differentiate hierarchies of size.
Able to calculate distances on a map, knowing the scale.

A
Able to use the European Studies Library.
Able to use lines of latitude and longitude to locate cities etc. on a map.
Able to prepare a simple questionnaire.
Able to conduct a simple interview.
Has acquired other skills on own through extended study.

A & C
Able to use and interpret diagrams and illustrations for information.
Able to follow oral and written instructions.
Able to recall material.
Able to find information accurately from a mass of material.
Able to produce clear written work.
Able to use correct punctuation (Capital Letters, Commas, Full Stops etc.)

BEHAVIOUR

Cheerful.	Co-operative.
Usually polite.	Sometimes insolent.
Noisy.	Never needs correction.
Rearely needs correction.	Quiet – reserved.
Disruptive.	Often needs correction.
Always polite.	Constantly needs correction.
Talkative.	Exceedingly co-operative and helpful.
Pleasant – gets on with others.	Resentful and unhelpful.
Sometimes noisy.	Confident.
Can be talkative.	Can be disruptive.

ORAL CONTRIBUTION IN LESSONS

Has difficulty taking part in discussions.
Takes an active part in class discussions.
Reluctant to take part in discussions.
Takes part in class discussions when prompted.

OTHER COMMENTS

PUPIL'S COMMENTS

PARENT'S COMMENTS

Teacher's Signature—————— Pupil's Signature——————

Date——————   Date——————

Parent's Signature——————

Date——————

END OF YEAR SUMMARY

Grade A = 135–150; Grade B = 115–134; Grade C = 85–114; Grade D = 55–84;
Grade E–Below 55.

Examination Result   /150   A.   B.   C.   D.   E.

COMMENT ON EXAMINATION RESULT

Must read the questions carefully in future.
Needs to revise thoroughly in future.
Not as good as expected.
Excellent.
Needs to allocate examination time with more care.
Poor.
Better than expected.
Good.
As expected.
Very good.
Satisfactory.

FINAL COMMENT ON YEAR'S WORK

PUPIL'S COMMENT

PARENT'S COMMENT

Teacher's Signature—————— Pupil's Signature——————

Date——————   Date——————

Parent's Signature——————

Date——————

Further Reading

A detailed bibliography, including reference to specialist articles in educational journals, is provided at the end of each chapter. More general works, which teachers should find both useful and easily available, include:

GENERAL

Bruner, J., *The process of education*. Harvard, 1960
Bruner, J., *Towards a theory of instruction*. Harvard, 1966
Deale, R. N., *Assessment and testing in the secondary school*. Evans/Methuen, 1975
Frith, D. S. and Macintosh, H. G., *A teacher's guide to assessment*. Stanley Thornes, 1984
Hargreaves, D., *The challenge for the comprehensive school*. Routledge & Kegan Paul, 1982
Kelly, A. V., *The curriculum: theory and practice*. Harper and Row, 1977
Reid, M. et al, *Mixed ability teaching: problems and possibilities*. NFER, 1981
Shipman, M. D., *In-school evaluation*. Heinemann, 1979

REMEDIAL/SPECIAL EDUCATION

Ainscow, M. and Tweddle, D., *Preventing classroom failure: the objectives approach*. John Wiley, 1979
Brennan, W., *Shaping the education of slow learners*. Routledge & Kegan Paul, 1974
Brennan, W., *Curricular needs of slow learners*. Evans/Methuen, 1979
Brennan, W., *Changing special education*. Open University Press, 1982
Gains, C. and McNicholas, J. (eds.), *Remedial education: guidelines for the future*. Longman, 1975
Griffin, D., *Slow learners: a break in the circle*. Woburn, 1978
Hinson, M. (ed.), *Encouraging results*. Macdonald, 1978
Hinson, M. and Hughes, M. (eds.), *Planning effective progress*. Hulton, 1982
Holt, J., *How children fail*. Penguin, 1964
Tansley, A. E. and Gulliford, R., *The education of slow-learning children*. Routledge & Kegan Paul, 1960
Tansley, P. and Panckhurst, J., *Children with specific learning difficulties*. NFER, 1981
Weber, K. J., *Yes, they can: a practical guide for teaching the adolescent slow learner*. Open University Press, 1978
Warnock Report, *Special educational needs*. HMSO, 1978

LANGUAGE

Bullock Report, *A Language for life*. HMSO, 1975
Harrison, C., *Readability in the classroom*. Cambridge University Press, 1980

Levine, N., *Language, teaching and learning: History.* Ward Lock, 1981
Lunzer, E. and Gardner, K. (eds.), *The effective use of reading.* Heinemann, 1979
Marland, M., *Language across the curriculum.* Heinemann, 1977
Martin, N. et al, *Writing and learning across the curriculum* 11–16. Ward Lock, 1976

HISTORY TEACHING

Adams, A. and Jones, E., *Teaching humanities in the microelectronic age.* Open University Press, 1983
Coltham, J. and Fines, J., *Educational objectives for the study of history.* Historical Association, 1971
Cowie, E., *History and the slow-learning child.* Historical Association, 1979
Dickinson, A. L. and Lee, P. J. (eds.), *History teaching and historical understanding.* Heinemann, 1978
Garvey, B. and Krug, M., *Models of history teaching in the secondary school.* Oxford, 1977
Gunning, D., *The teaching of history.* Croom Helm, 1978
Hodgkinson, K., *Designing a history syllabus for slow-learning children.* Historical Association, (n.d.)
Hunt, J. W. (ed.), *Computers in secondary school history teaching.* Historical Association, 1979
ILEA, *History and social sciences at secondary level – Part Two: History,* 1982
Jones, G. and Ward, L. (eds.), *New History, Old Problems* Swansea 1978
Mays, P., *Why teach history?* London, 1974
McIver, V. (ed.), *Teaching history to slow-learning children in secondary schools.* Belfast, 1982
New South Wales Dept. of Ed., *Curriculum ideas: catering for the slow learner – History.* Sydney, 1981
Nichol, J. D., *Simulation in history teaching.* Historical Association, 1980
Reeves, M., *Why History?* Longman, 1980
Rogers, P. J., *The new history: theory into practice.* Historical Association, 1979
Unwin, R., *The visual dimension in the study and teaching of history.* Historical Association, 1981
Watts, D. G., *The learning of history.* Routledge & Kegan Paul, 1972

Index